GREAT LIVES OBSERVED

Gerald Emanuel Stearn, *General Editor*

EACH VOLUME IN THE SERIES VIEWS THE CHARACTER AND ACHIEVEMENT OF A GREAT WORLD FIGURE IN THREE PERSPECTIVES—THROUGH HIS OWN WORDS, THROUGH THE OPINIONS OF HIS CONTEMPORARIES, AND THROUGH RETROSPECTIVE JUDGMENTS—THUS COMBINING THE INTIMACY OF AUTOBIOGRAPHY, THE IMMEDIACY OF EYEWITNESS OBSERVATION, AND THE OBJECTIVITY OF MODERN SCHOLARSHIP.

E. DAVID CRONON, the editor of this volume in the Great Lives Observed series, is Professor of History and Director of the Institute for Research in the Humanities at the University of Wisconsin at Madison. He has written widely on various aspects of twentieth-century American history and is the author of the first scholarly biography of Marcus Garvey, *Black Moses: the Story of Marcus Garvey and the Universal Negro Improvement Association* (1955).

GREAT LIVES OBSERVED

MARCUS GARVEY

GREAT LIVES OBSERVED

Marcus Garvey

Edited by E. DAVID CRONON

*Be assured that I planted well the
seed of Negro or black nationalism
which cannot be destroyed even by the
foul play that has been meted out to me.*
—MARCUS GARVEY
First message from Atlanta Penitentiary, 1925

A SPECTRUM BOOK

PRENTICE-HALL, INC., ENGLEWOOD CLIFFS, N.J.

Library of Congress Cataloging in Publication Data

CRONON, EDMUND DAVID, comp.
    Marcus Garvey.

    (Great lives observed)   (A Spectrum Book)
    Bibliography: p.
    1. Garvey, Marcus, 1887–1940.
E185.97.G3C72   1973   301.45′19′6024   [B]
ISBN 0–13–556068–3   73–9796
ISBN 0–13–556050–0 (pbk.)

Cover credit: United Press International

© 1973 by PRENTICE-HALL, INC.,
Englewood Cliffs, N.J.

A SPECTRUM BOOK

10 9 8 7 6 5 4 3 2 1

Printed in the United States of America

PRENTICE-HALL INTERNATIONAL, INC. (*London*)
PRENTICE-HALL OF AUSTRALIA PTY., LTD. (*Sydney*)
PRENTICE-HALL OF CANADA, LTD. (*Toronto*)
PRENTICE-HALL OF INDIA PRIVATE LIMITED (*New Delhi*)
PRENTICE-HALL OF JAPAN, INC. (*Tokyo*)

Contents

Introduction **1**

Chronology of the Life of Marcus Garvey **17**

PART ONE
GARVEY LOOKS AT THE WORLD

1

From Jamaica to New York **19**

Letter to Dr. Booker T. Washington: April 12, 1915, *23*
Manifesto of the Universal Negro Improvement Association, *24*

2

Garvey Maxims **27**

3

Declaration of Rights of the Negro Peoples of
 the World **30**

4

Building Race Pride **38**

History and the Negro, *38* Miscegenation, *39* Purity of
Race, *40* Race Assimilation, *40* Race Purity a Desideratum, *41* The Image of God, *41*

5

For a New Negro Press **43**

The "Colored" or Negro Press, *43*

6

Redeeming the African Motherland **47**

vii

7

Garvey's Message for Whites   **51**

Aims and Objects of Movement for Solution of Negro Problem, *51*   The Spiritual Brotherhood of Man, *52*   Supplying a Long-Felt Want, *53*   Negroes Who Seek Social Equality, *54*

8

Advice to Black Workers   **57**

The Negro, Communism, Trade Unionism, and His (?) Friend: "Beware of Greeks Bearing Gifts," *57*

9

The Collapse of Garvey's Dream   **61**

Closing Address to the Jury, *61*   First Message to the Negroes of the World from Atlanta Prison, *66*

10

Keeping the Faith   **69**

The American Negro, *69*   Senator Bilbo's Bill, *70*

PART TWO

THE WORLD LOOKS AT GARVEY

11

A New Nation in Harlem   **73**

12

DuBois Asks Some Searching Questions   **80**

13

Garvey's Message Reaches Africa   **89**

14

British and French Apprehension   92

To Lord Curzon, *92*

15

African Suspicion   94

16

An Answer to Garvey's Appeal to White America   97

Major Cox's Letter, *98*   With Marcus Garvey at Atlanta, *98*   The Negro Is Awake, *99*   The South Does Not Hate the Negro, *100*

17

Robert W. Bagnall: The Madness of Marcus Garvey   102

Is Garvey a Paranoiac?, *103*   False Imagination, *104*   Unduly Suspicious, *105*   "Castles in Spain," *106*

18

George Alexander McGuire: "Garvey's Work Shall Endure Throughout the Ages"   107

19

Should the Garvey Movement Be Saved or Destroyed?   112

Salvage the U.N.I.A.: A Communist View, *112*   Destroy the U.N.I.A.: A Socialist View, *117*

20

E. Franklin Frazier: Garvey as a Mass Leader   118

PART THREE
GARVEY IN HISTORY

21

James Weldon Johnson: Glitter Instead of Substance   123

22
Robert Hughes Brisbane, Jr.: Building Black
Self-Esteem   126

23
Ben F. Rogers: DuBois and Garvey   130

24
Theodore G. Bilbo: A Divine Afflatus   135

25
Robert G. Weisbord: Garvey's Ultimate Victory   141

26
George Shepperson: Garvey as Pan-Africanist   144

27
Jabez Ayodele Langley: Garvey and African
Nationalism   148

28
Rupert Lewis: Garveyism in Jamaica   154

29
The Republic of Cameroon: An African Tribute   161

To Mrs. Amy Jacques Garvey, *161*

30
Clarence Harding: Continuing Garvey's Work in
Africa   163

Afterword: An Enduring Legacy   167

Bibliographical Note   170

Index   173

For Amy Jacques Garvey
Indefatigable Champion of Human Rights

Introduction

On March 23, 1916, an obscure young black man named Marcus Garvey arrived in Harlem from his native Jamaica. This was his first visit to the United States, though some years earlier he had traveled throughout Central America and the Caribbean and had lived for eighteen months in England. Short, stocky, largely self-educated, a gifted writer and superb orator, Garvey was brimming with messianic fervor to unite and uplift the oppressed blacks not only in his island homeland but also throughout the world. Over the next few years he created the first real mass movement among American Negroes, an astonishing feat for an upstart foreigner and one that has yet to be duplicated. Although Garvey's greatest following was in the United States, his movement was active on three continents, and his black nationalist ideas stirred the imagination of Negroes everywhere, from Africa to Australia. At the peak of his influence in the early 1920s, his following probably numbered in the millions. The Garvey movement as an organized force flourished for little more than a decade, and at the time of his death in 1940, Marcus Garvey was living in obscurity in London, largely forgotten by the black masses he had once led. Yet after Garvey the Negro world would never be the same.

There was nothing about Garvey's early life to suggest that he would one day command worldwide attention. He was born on August 17, 1887 in the peaceful little town of St. Ann's Bay, on Jamaica's northern coast. His parents named him Marcus after his father, and tradition has it that his mother, Sarah, sought to give him the middle name of Moses in the hope that, like the biblical Moses, he would grow up to lead his people. His father, a far-from-devout stonemason, objected, and the parents compromised with Mosiah. Both Sarah and Marcus Garvey were of unmixed Negro stock, with the father said to be descended from the Maroons, the escaped African slaves whose fierce guerrilla warfare in defense of their freedom in the mountains of Jamaica had defied both Spanish and British attempts at their subjugation. Garvey's later stress upon racial purity probably was derived as much from pride in his Maroon heritage as from his humiliating experience as a full-blooded black man in the Jamaican three-color caste system, in which the small mulatto group was accorded special privileges and influence by the tiny white ruling class.

Young Marcus attended the elementary school in St. Ann's Bay and may have had some additional work at the local Anglican grammar

1

school. He also read as widely as he could, starting first with the books of his father, who, though largely self-educated, was locally respected for his learning and his private library. Family financial difficulties forced Garvey to leave school at the age of fourteen to become a printer's apprentice, training which helped to sharpen the journalistic skills that were later to be so important in the development of his movement. At seventeen he moved across the island to the capital city of Kingston to work at his new trade. Here he also developed an interest in public speaking, visiting various churches to observe the delivery of the most effective Kingston preachers, practicing for hours before the mirror in his room, and taking an increasingly active part in street meetings. In 1907 Garvey participated in a printers' strike, which eventually failed when the employers introduced linotype machines operated by imported printers and the union's treasurer absconded with the remaining strike funds. Garvey later claimed that he was blacklisted for his leadership of the strike, though it seems questionable that at twenty he had achieved a key role in one of the oldest Jamaican trade unions. Nevertheless, the experience seems to have left him thereafter contemptuous of labor unions and their ability to solve the problems of black workers.

Over the next few years he held a variety of jobs and grew increasingly interested in reform activities. He traveled about the Caribbean and in Central America, working for a time on a United Fruit banana plantation in Costa Rica and on newspapers in Port Limón and Colón. Depressed conditions had led a sizable number of Jamaican blacks like Garvey to leave the island in search of work, and everywhere he found his black countrymen and other Negroes subject to humiliating discrimination and exploitation. Yet when Garvey indignantly sought the aid of British consular authorities, he found them quite indifferent to the mistreatment of blacks, whether or not they were British subjects. He concluded that black people would never be able to count on justice or equal treatment from whites.

In 1912 Garvey went to London, where he probably took some courses at Birkbeck College, a school for workers, which is now a part of the University of London. For the first time he had a chance to meet native Africans—students, sailors, dock workers, and others—and to learn firsthand about conditions in Africa and other parts of the British Empire. He was greatly influenced by a scholarly Egyptian nationalist, Duse Mohammed Ali, who gave him a chance to write for his *Africa Times and Orient Review*. The dark-skinned Duse Mohammed bitterly resented the insidious British color bar and as an ardent anticolonialist fired Garvey's interest in the cause of African freedom. It was in London, too, that Garvey first became interested in the condition of Negroes in the United States. He came across a copy of

Booker T. Washington's autobiography and was profoundly affected by its stress upon Negro self-help. He later recalled:

> I read *Up from Slavery* by Booker T. Washington, and then my doom —if I may so call it—of being a race leader dawned upon me. . . . I asked: "Where is the black man's Government? Where is his King and his kingdom? Where is his President, his country, and his ambassador, his army, his navy, his men of big affairs?" I could not find them, and then I declared, "I will help to make them." [1]

When Garvey returned home in 1914, he was full of ambitious plans to uplift Jamaican blacks and to unite the scattered Negroes of the world. Enlisting the support of a small group of old friends, on August 1, 1914, he established the organization that would henceforth be his life's work. Its imposing title, the Universal Negro Improvement and Conservation Association and African Communities League (usually shortened to the first words and abbreviated as U.N.I.A.) suggested Garvey's broad objective of "drawing the peoples of the race together" through a varied program of education, promotion of race pride, worldwide commercial and industrial intercourse, and development of the African motherland. The first U.N.I.A. project was a Jamaican agricultural and industrial school modeled after Booker T. Washington's Tuskegee Institute. The proposal won support from some influential whites, including the colonial governor and the mayor of Kingston, but to Garvey's dismay the blacks were largely apathetic and the mulatto group openly hostile to anything that seemed to threaten its privileged status. Hoping for a warmer response among American Negroes, Garvey wrote Washington and received an invitation to visit Tuskegee during his planned lecture tour in the United States. But before he could complete his travel arrangements late in 1915, Washington was dead, and with him died Garvey's best hope for an influential American sponsor.

Black America was undergoing profound social change when Marcus Garvey, alone and unknown, arrived in New York in the spring of 1916. For Garvey these fortuitous developments would spell the difference between success and likely failure, since they would help to produce a receptive audience for his message of race redemption. The First World War had created a sharply rising demand for American manufactures while virtually halting the traditional flow of European immigrant labor into Northern factories. The resulting labor shortage was met in part by black and white migrants from Southern cotton

---

[1] Marcus Garvey, "The Negro's Greatest Enemy," in Amy Jacques Garvey, ed., *Philosophy and Opinions of Marcus Garvey*, vol. II (New York: Universal Publishing House, 1926), p. 126.

fields, who were suffering both from curtailed wartime markets and from the disastrous effects of the spread of the boll weevil over large areas of the Cotton Belt at this time. During the years 1916–18, perhaps half a million Southern Negroes moved to the North in search of better jobs and living conditions, with some Northern cities experiencing a phenomenal increase in the number and proportion of their black residents.

The North, however, hardly proved a promised land for most of the black migrants. Sharp competition for jobs and housing led to rising tension and occasional interracial clashes in a number of cities during the war. Nor did America's wartime crusade for democracy measure up to the initial high expectations of black citizens. Negroes were not accepted for service in the navy except as mess attendants, while blacks who volunteered or were drafted into the army often experienced humiliating discriminatory treatment. Those who served overseas with the American Expeditionary Force could not help but contrast their Jim Crow status at home with the ready acceptance they found in a more tolerant French society. These social pressures crested in the summer of 1919, when an economic slump resulting from the abrupt postwar demobilization helped to fuel a wave of bloody race riots across the nation, the worst in its history. For many blacks, disillusionment with white America was now complete. Deeply discouraged, yet proud, angry, even defiant, they were in no mood to slip quietly back into their pre-war second-class status. On the contrary, they were ready for a black Moses whose words would bolster their battered self-respect and whose program would promise a way for Negroes to build their own bright future, free from white domination. Equally ready for the task was Marcus Garvey, the magnetic young leader of the fledgling Universal Negro Improvement Association.

During 1916 and 1917 Garvey traveled extensively throughout the United States, speaking to Negro audiences about the exciting challenge of race redemption. He was sufficiently encouraged about the warmth of his response to establish an American branch of the U.N.I.A. in Harlem, where the sizable West Indian immigrant community provided him with the nucleus of his initial American following. Thereafter, until his deportation in 1927, Garvey made Harlem and the United States the headquarters of what was increasingly a worldwide movement. Details of Garvey's early proselytizing efforts in the United States are obscure, but he claimed by 1919 to have visited thirty-eight states, advocating black unity and organizing new divisions of the U.N.I.A. His powerful personality and platform eloquence enabled him to surmount at least two early challenges to his leadership of the New York U.N.I.A. by rival West Indian organizers and Harlem politicians. It was soon clear that Marcus Garvey was the dominant force in the rapidly growing movement and was in fact essential to its continued development.

Recognizing the need to keep in continued touch with his scattered following, in January 1918 Garvey began publication of a newspaper, the *Negro World,* which quickly became one of the leading American black weeklies and a most effective vehicle for the promotion of Garveyism. In its heyday the *Negro World* had a regular circulation of at least 50,000, and a readership in the United States and abroad no doubt several times that number. The paper was well-edited with a characteristically lively style, for Garvey attracted to its staff at one time or another a number of black journalists who had themselves been editors of newspapers or magazines. The bulk of each issue was written in English, but there were usually sections in French and Spanish for its Negro readers in Africa, the West Indies, and Latin America. Each issue of the *Negro World* carried a lengthy front-page editorial by Garvey addressed to the "Fellowmen of the Negro Race," which reminded readers of their proud history—especially the glories of ancient African civilizations—and called upon them to work for a bright future under the red, black, and green banner of the U.N.I.A. Garvey extolled the beauty of black skin and pure negroid features, and refused to accept advertisements that tended to degrade the race, such as skin-whitening and hair-straightening compounds. Instead, the paper pushed the sale of black dolls, a new toy development reflecting the rising sense of race pride among Negroes. As proclaimed on its masthead, the *Negro World* was "A Newspaper Devoted Solely to the Interests of the Negro Race."

During 1919 and 1920 Garvey's Universal Negro Improvement Association grew spectacularly, fed by Negro disillusionment with the empty promise of America as reflected in the wave of bloody race riots throughout the country in the summer of 1919. "Up, you mighty race!" Garvey thundered. "You can accomplish what you will." [2] And the black masses responded by the thousands. New U.N.I.A. divisions were chartered in most American cities with a significant Negro population. Members paid a dollar initially and thereafter monthly dues of thirty-five cents, of which ten cents went to Garvey's international headquarters in New York. By the summer of 1919 Garvey had raised enough money to purchase a large auditorium—the roofed-over basement of an unfinished Harlem church—which he renamed Liberty Hall. At the dedication ceremonies he reminded his audience of the shameful race riot in Washington only days before, which had made a mockery of the nation's shrines to liberty and justice for all. Liberty Hall in New York, and its counterparts which soon appeared in other cities, would

[2] Quoted in Claude McKay, *Harlem: Negro Metropolis* (New York: Dutton, 1940), p. 154.

henceforth be the headquarters of the crusade for race redemption, bastions of black freedom.

Early in 1919 Garvey began to speak prophetically of a fleet of black-owned and -operated steamships that would link the Negro peoples of the world, uniting the black diaspora of the New World with the African motherland. The daring proposal quickly captured the popular imagination, and for several months the U.N.I.A. collected money to purchase ships for this promised Black Star Line. Warned by a New York district attorney not to sell stock unless the enterprise was organized as a legitimate business, on June 16, 1919, Garvey formally launched the Black Star Line under a broad charter of incorporation from the State of Delaware, whose lenient laws required little more than a filing fee. Capitalized initially at $500,000 (subsequently raised to $10 million for an additional registration fee in February 1920), with shares modestly priced at five dollars and limited to Negroes, the new company, so a B.S.L. circular promised, offered "to every Black Man, Woman, and Child the opportunity to climb the great ladder of industrial and commercial progress." [3]

At first the audacious scheme was laughed off by many Negroes as just another attempt to extort money from the unsophisticated black masses. But in mid-September 1919, Garvey proudly announced that the first ship of the new line could be viewed at her 135th Street berth. The vessel was the *S.S. Yarmouth,* a small steamship of only 1,452 gross tons that had been built in 1887, the year of Garvey's birth. The *Yarmouth*'s value was more symbolic than commercial, for the squat little ship, still grimy from its most recent cargo of coal, was hardly a promising entry into international maritime trade. It had, moreover, cost a steep $165,000, and its antiquated machinery promised to eat up thousands more dollars of scarce B.S.L. capital. No matter; the black world was mightily impressed with the achievement of this daring Jamaican who had accomplished something unique in race history. Two months later thousands of Negroes turned out for the departure of the *Yarmouth* on its maiden voyage to the West Indies under the red, black, and green flag of the Black Star Line. Hundreds paid a dollar to go aboard to watch the smart Negro crew, under its black captain, Joshua Cockbourne, make ready to cast off. Blacks everywhere, even in remote parts of Africa, took vicarious pride in the actuality of a steamship operated by a Negro company and manned by a black captain and crew. Sales of Black Star stock boomed, and a recording company even issued a phonograph record of a popular song entitled "Black Star Line."

Garvey quickly followed this triumph by buying two additional

[3] *Garvey* v. *U.S.,* no. 8317, Ct. App., 2d Cir., Feb. 2, 1925, pp. 2474–75; W. E. B. DuBois, "Marcus Garvey," *Crisis* 21 (January, 1921): 113.

ships for the line in the spring of 1920. One, the *S.S. Shadyside,* was a Hudson River excursion boat built in 1873. Purchased for $35,000, the *Shadyside* was intended for use by U.N.I.A. members on summer excursions, as well as for B.S.L. promotional activities. The other vessel was the steam yacht *Kanawha,* formerly owned by Standard Oil magnate Henry H. Rogers, which the line purchased for $60,000 plus an additional $25,000 for refitting for passenger and light cargo service in the West Indies. There was general rejoicing at the first annual meeting of the stockholders of the Black Star Line held on July 20, 1920, in Liberty Hall, which was jammed to capacity. The crowd expressed awe when it learned that the line had raised through stock sales and subscriptions a working capital amounting to the impressive sum of $610,-860. True, the three B.S.L. ships were hardly giant liners, Garvey conceded, but "we were satisfied to purchase small boats so as to show that we can run them." In any event, he declared, the work of the past year was of great benefit to Negroes everywhere, "for it has brought recognition to us as a race—it has elevated our men." In their jubilation the stockholders could be forgiven their failure to notice an unexplained item in the treasurer's report listed cryptically as "organization expense" and totaling $289,066.[4]

The Black Star Line was but one of Marcus Garvey's imaginative schemes for leading his people along the road to economic independence and self-respect. In 1919 he also established the Negro Factories Corporation, capitalized at one million dollars under a Delaware charter. Offering stock to Negroes at five dollars a share, the company planned to provide loans and executive or technical assistance to Negroes who needed help in establishing their own small businesses. In practice, the corporation usually lacked funds to lend to ambitious black entrepreneurs, but it helped to develop a chain of cooperative grocery stores, a restaurant, steam laundry, tailor and dressmaking shop, millinery store, and publishing house. Negroes must create their own economic opportunities, Garvey advised, for "a race without authority and power, is a race without respect."[5]

Late in 1919 Garvey issued a call for the first international convention of the Universal Negro Improvement Association, with delegates representing all parts of the black world, to be held in New York during August 1920. The *Negro World* proclaimed that the gathering would be the largest of its kind in the history of the race, and Garvey and his lieutenants devoted months of careful planning and promotion to make it so. Judged by any standards, this 1920 convention was a spectacular affair, marking perhaps the high point of the Garvey

---

[4] *Garvey v. U.S.,* pp. 2653–56.
[5] Amy Jacques Garvey, ed., *Philosophy and Opinions of Marcus Garvey, op. cit.,* vol. I (1923), p. 2.

movement. The several thousand black delegates came from all forty-eight American states and more than a score of countries on three continents. Even though colonial authorities had banned the *Negro World* in French and parts of British Africa, there were a number of African delegates, including a native prince, several tribal chiefs, and the mayor of Monrovia, Liberia. The convention opened on Sunday, August 1, with three religious services and a silent march of members and delegates through the streets of Harlem. This was but a prelude for the huge parade the next afternoon, which was the talk of Harlem for months to come. For the first time all of the components and massed units of the U.N.I.A. were revealed to an astonished and admiring black world. In addition to numerous bands, choruses, and contingents from the various local U.N.I.A. divisions, there were units of the new African Legion, smartly dressed in dark blue uniforms with red-striped trousers, some mounted on horseback and others marching with well-drilled precision. Although the Legionnaires were unarmed except for the dress swords of their officers, many were veterans of the recent World War, and their existence as a paramilitary organization suggested that Garvey believed the redemption of the race might require force. Another uniformed group was the Black Cross Nurses, neatly garbed in white, ready to back their men in the African Legion or aid stricken peoples anywhere in the world. The parade, stretching several miles through Harlem, was an impressive show of organizational strength, and for the first time the white press began to take notice of Marcus Garvey.

More significant was the fierce black nationalism that pervaded every meeting of the month-long convention. "We are the descendants of a suffering people," declared Garvey, clad in a richly colored academic cap and gown, to twenty-five thousand of his followers massed in Madison Square Garden for the opening business session:

> We are the descendants of a people determined to suffer no longer. We shall now organize the 400,000,000 Negroes of the world into a vast organization to plant the banner of freedom on the great continent of Africa. . . . If Europe is for the Europeans, then Africa shall be for the black peoples of the world. We say it; we mean it.[6]

Responding to the call for liberation of the African motherland, the convention designated Garvey as the Provisional President of the African Republic, a kind of government-in-exile. The delegates also adopted a sweeping Declaration of the Rights of the Negro Peoples of the World. Developed after nearly two weeks of reports on the problems and mistreatment of blacks in all parts of the world, the

[6] *The New York Times*, August 3, 1920.

Declaration was both a powerful protest and comprehensive program of action, much of which remains valid today. When the convention adjourned at the end of August 1920, Harlem was both exhausted and exhilarated. It was clear that Garveyism was a potent new force in race relations. For the first time in the long centuries since their ancestors had left Africa in chains, masses of Negroes in the United States and elsewhere in the New World were glorying in their color, confident of their latent power and bright future. To many, Marcus Garvey and his Universal Negro Improvement Association seemed to offer the means for the unification and regeneration of the black world.

Garvey's growing emphasis on black separatism and nationalism demanded a reorientation in religion as well. In 1921 he organized the African Orthodox Church, headed by Bishop George Alexander McGuire, a former Episcopalian clergyman who had joined the U.N.I.A. as chaplain general. The new Negro church, Garvey and McGuire declared, would be true to the teachings of Christ without the hypocrisy of the white churches. Garvey urged his followers to conceive of a multiracial heaven and to think of Christ as embodying all races, black no less than white. By 1924 Bishop McGuire was advising Garveyites to replace their portraits of a white Madonna and Child with appropriately black figures; henceforth, he noted wryly, only the Negro's devil would be white, instead of the traditional black.

The stress upon African redemption at the 1920 convention also signaled a new and more ambitious thrust of the Garvey movement. Even before the convention, Garvey had sent a delegation to Liberia, the only independent black state on the African continent, to scout the possibilities for a U.N.I.A. development project there. Liberia seemed the most promising base for any U.N.I.A. activities aimed at liberating the African motherland. Its finances in chronic disarray, the Liberian government welcomed any financial aid from American Negroes, and its leaders, the descendants of American slaves repatriated to Africa in the nineteenth century, promised their full cooperation. Late in 1920 Garvey launched a drive for a two-million-dollar construction loan to rehabilitate Liberia. Early the following year he sent a group of black technicians to staff what amounted to a U.N.I.A. legation in Monrovia and to lay the groundwork for a future colonization project. President Edwin J. Barclay gave assurances of Liberia's willingness to provide lands for U.N.I.A. colonists, but he cautioned against too much publicity for the project, noting that the British and French governments had expressed concern about his government's involvement with the U.N.I.A. By this time Garvey's *Negro World* was banned in most of black Africa, and colonial authorities were keeping a close watch for U.N.I.A. organizers. Among Garvey's followers in the New World, interest in Africa remained high, however, and by its second annual convention in August 1921, the U.N.I.A. had raised more than $137,000 for the Liberian development loan. Unfortunately, Garvey was obliged to divert most of these funds to meet unexpectedly heavy operating expenses of the Black Star Line, and as a result only a tiny and intermittent trickle of money and supplies went to the U.N.I.A. mission in Liberia.

For the Black Star Line was proving to be a financial and operational disaster. Much of the difficulty was attributable to the inexperience of Garvey and his associates in managing an enterprise as complex as the U.N.I.A. and its component parts had suddenly become. Garvey considered himself the leader of a broad-gauged uplift movement, not simply a business venture. He consequently used funds collected for various U.N.I.A. projects interchangeably as the need arose, without establishing careful accounting procedures and records. While he talked of the Black Star Line as a noble vehicle to link the Negro peoples of the world in commercial intercourse, he used it primarily as a promotional tool, with its ships dispatched more to stimulate stock sales and U.N.I.A. membership than to earn operating revenue by carrying cargo and passengers. Even well-established steamship companies with ample capital resources or government backing faced serious competitive pressures after the war. The Black Star Line, with meager financing, a small and obsolete fleet, and inexperienced personnel afloat and ashore, was a risky venture at best, and by 1921 the Line was in desperate straits. The *Yarmouth*, flagship of the Black Star fleet, ran aground twice and suffered numerous mechanical breakdowns on its three voyages to the West Indies, before being sold ignominiously at a court-ordered auction for a paltry $1,625 late in 1921. In two years the rusty little ship had swallowed up $194,803 of Black Star funds. The excursion steamer *Shadyside* made a number of trips up the Hudson River during the summer of 1920, but during the following winter she sprang a seam during a bad ice storm and sank. By this time the line was in no condition to attempt a salvage operation to retrieve its twenty-thousand-dollar capital investment. Nor was this advisable, for the inefficient *Shadyside* had cost eleven thousand dollars in operating losses during its five months of active B.S.L. service. The record of the *Kanawha*, the only ship for which the line ever completed payment, was just as dismal. Ater a number of breakdowns necessitating expensive repairs, the *Kanawha* finally reached the West Indies in the spring of 1921 and toured the Caribbean promoting the U.N.I.A. The ship continued to require costly repairs, however, and finally was abandoned at Antilla, Cuba, several months later, its hapless crew shipped home at the expense of the U.S. government. In addition to its purchase price of sixty thousand dollars, the *Kanawha* in less than a year and a half consumed a staggering total of $134,681 of B.S.L. funds while taking in only $1,207 of operating revenue.

Meanwhile, Garvey tried desperately to keep the Black Star flag afloat, well aware of its symbolic value to his crusade for Negro unity and African redemption. To avoid the mounting debts of the old Black Star Line of Delaware, and to facilitate the acquisition of a larger ship for trade with West Africa, late in 1920 he quietly obtained a charter from New Jersey for a new Black Star Steamship Company. Over the next year the new corporation sought unsuccessfully to obtain a suitable ship from the United States Shipping Board, tying up a deposit of $22,500 in tangled legal negotiations. Rumors of Black Star mismanagement and operating difficulties, as well as Garvey's failure to produce the long-promised *Phyllis Wheatley* for the African route, fed growing doubts and criticism within and outside the ranks of the U.N.I.A. Much of the Negro establishment in the United States had long resented the success of this Jamaican upstart, and from late 1920 onward they launched an increasingly bitter attack against the U.N.I.A. leader's shaky business activities. In response to this editorial criticism as well as to complaints from a few disgruntled B.S.L. stockholders, early in 1922 federal authorities arrested and indicted Garvey and three of his associates for fraudulent use of the mails in promoting the sale of Black Star stock. With no ships in operation and a cash balance of only $31.12, Garvey could but announce sadly, "We have suspended the activities of the Black Star Line." [7]

Even in adversity, Garvey retained an impressive following among the black masses. Despite some factionalism, the 1922 convention revealed that the ranks of the U.N.I.A. were largely intact, with an overwhelming majority of the membership accepting their leader's bitter account of the dishonesty and treachery that had brought about the collapse of the Black Star Line. The faithful were confident that Garvey's noble objectives would be recognized at his mail-fraud trial, which got under way in May of 1923. Garvey conducted his own defense, using the courtroom as a forum not only to defend his management of the bankrupt steamship company but also to explain his dream of providing badly needed self-respect and economic opportunity for his downtrodden race. Government accountants had little trouble showing that the Black Star Line had raised more than three-quarters of a million dollars through the sale of 155,510 shares of stock to nearly forty thousand Negroes, and that this impressive achievement had been squandered on dubious capital assets and ruinous operating deficits. Yet the prosecution's case rested on the ques-

[7] *Negro World,* April 1, 1922.

tionable assumption that Garvey and his codefendants had knowingly and with criminal intent used the mails to promote stock sales after they were aware that the line's financial condition was hopeless. Here the evidence was at best mixed. Although some of Garvey's subordinates had, moreover, clearly profited by their connection with the line, neither he nor his codefendants had accepted lavish salaries or exorbitant expenses for their work. The Black Star Line might have been an ill-advised and even foolish venture, but there was nothing to suggest that it had been intended as anything but a broadly based Negro-improvement effort. Garvey's often brash and seemingly arrogant courtroom conduct probably influenced the jury against him, however, for it found him guilty while acquitting his fellow defendants. The judge, a white member of the National Association for the Advancement of Colored People, declared his full agreement, and sternly sentenced the U.N.I.A. leader to the maximum term of five years in prison and a fine of a thousand dollars. "My work is just begun," Garvey asserted proudly, "and as I lay down my life for the cause of my people, so do I feel that succeeding generations shall be inspired by the sacrifice that I made for the rehabilitation of our race." [8] Undaunted, his loyal followers raised twenty-five thousand dollars for bail while his attorneys appealed the verdict.

While awaiting the outcome of his appeal, in 1924 the irrepressible Garvey launched yet another maritime venture, the Black Cross Navigation and Trading Company. The corporation promptly made a firm offer to purchase at least one ship from the U.S. Shipping Board, which still held the Black Star Line's $22,500 deposit, but the Board declined to do business with the new Garvey enterprise. Garvey thereupon acquired the *General G.W. Goethals,* a larger and much sounder ship than the ill-fated *Yarmouth,* from the Panama Railroad Company. He announced that the ship would be rechristened the *Booker T. Washington* and that its purchase had been made possible by the sale of Black Cross stock to 3,600 loyal members of the association. The new Black Cross flagship was the hit of the U.N.I.A.'s 1924 convention and seemed to the faithful ample proof of Garvey's continuing wisdom and invincibility. Even his detractors were momentarily stunned at this sudden turn in his fortunes.

Garvey probably hoped that the *Booker T. Washington* could be used to carry Negro colonists to Africa, for in June 1924 he dispatched an advance party of U.N.I.A. technical experts to lay out and construct four camps on lands earlier promised by the Liberian government at Cape Palmas. The U.N.I.A. also shipped a consignment of supplies and machinery worth fifty thousand dollars for the colonization project. Before the goods arrived in Liberia, however, they were attached

[8] Garvey, *Philosophy and Opinions,* vol. II, p. 218.

on complaint of the shipping company, which alleged that the U.N.I.A. had not made full payment. Eventually the shipment was confiscated by the Liberian custom service to cover storage charges. Nor did the U.N.I.A. advance party find a warmer welcome. Late in June the Liberian government abruptly announced that no Garveyites would be permitted to land in the African republic, and when the U.N.I.A. technicians arrived, they too were ignominiously seized and held for prompt deportation. The Liberian authorities evidently feared that the Garveyites would be a domestic political threat or might even jeopardize their nation's existence by antagonizing the British and French governments, whose neighboring colonies were trying to repress Garveyism. The bitterly disappointed delegates at the 1924 U.N.I.A. convention petitioned both the Liberian legislature and U.S. President Calvin Coolidge in protest, but for all practical purposes Liberia's unexpected hostility killed any Back to Africa movement. As a further insult, the following year the Liberian government included the erstwhile U.N.I.A. lands as part of a large rubber-development lease agreement with the Firestone Rubber Company.

The collapse of the Liberian colonization program was only a prelude to a further setback. Early in 1925 the United States Circuit Court of Appeals upheld Garvey's mail fraud conviction, and the Supreme Court declined to review the case. On February 8 the stocky U.N.I.A. president entered Atlanta penitentiary to begin serving his five-year sentence. His associates, led by his energetic and able second wife, Amy Jacques Garvey, whom he had married in 1922, tried to carry out his charge to keep the ranks of the Universal Negro Improvement Association intact, but without the magnetic leadership and inspiriting drive of its founder, the movement began to falter. The Black Cross flagship, the *General Goethals,* or *Booker T. Washington,* had to be sold at auction in 1926, marking the demise of this second Garvey maritime venture. Garvey's lieutenants called a special U.N.I.A. convention in Detroit in March 1926 to plan the association's program until his release, but they lacked his daring imagination and charismatic appeal. Local U.N.I.A. divisions mostly sought to hold their membership through rallies to promote Garvey's black nationalistic ideas and to urge clemency for their martyred leader. They were joined by a growing segment of the Negro press and the black community in general, which was increasingly persuaded that Marcus Garvey had been unjustly condemned and harshly treated by the white man's courts. In his adversity even those who had never embraced Garvey's philosophy now viewed him more sympathetically, and some saw his case as proof of his contention that America would never be a land of justice for blacks. No doubt in response to this mounting pressure, late in 1927 President Coolidge commuted Garvey's sentence and or-

dered him released. Because he was an alien who had been convicted of a felony, however, U.S. immigration laws required his immediate deportation. Without being permitted to visit his headquarters in New York, the U.N.I.A. leader was accordingly taken to New Orleans and put aboard the *S.S. Saramacca*, bound for Panama and the West Indies. Hundreds of his New Orleans followers turned out in the rain to hear his farewell address at the ship's rail before going into exile. "The greatest work is yet to be done," he promised. "I shall with God's help do it." [9]

Once back in his island homeland, Garvey launched an energetic drive to revitalize the neglected Jamaican association. He also toured the Caribbean and Central America, visiting local U.N.I.A. divisions and admonishing his followers to continue their work for the rehabilitation of the race. Well aware of the importance of his American legions in the movement, every week he cabled an editorial message for publication in the *Negro World*. In May of 1928 he and his wife traveled to Europe, establishing U.N.I.A. branch headquarters in London and Paris and addressing British and French audiences on the goals of his movement for Negro redemption. He also presented a second "Petition of the Negro Race" to the League of Nations at Geneva, demanding redress of a detailed list of grievances suffered by black people throughout the world. In particular, he urged the League to create a free Negro state in Africa, either through a mandate of the former German colonies on the continent or by bringing together parts of West Africa into a United Commonwealth of Black Nations. Ignored by the League, in the fall of 1928 he visited Canada, rashly advising his followers across the border to vote for the Democratic presidential candidate, Alfred E. Smith, in the coming election. The American consul in Montreal complained to Canadian authorities about this interference in his country's political affairs, and Garvey was summarily deported before he could complete his speaking engagements before U.N.I.A. groups in Ontario.

Determined to recreate the missionary fervor of the early days of the movement, Garvey issued a call for the Sixth International Convention of the Negro Peoples of the World to be held in Kingston, Jamaica, during the month of August 1929. This would turn out to be the last great U.N.I.A. convention, and in many respects it rivaled in size and splendor the first such gathering in Harlem in 1920. Again the emphasis was on African redemption, but the delegates spent long hours considering ways of improving Negro conditions throughout the New World as well. They voted to establish U.N.I.A. consulates in all important centers of black population to publicize grievances and

[9] Quoted in Len S. Nembhard, *Trials and Triumphs of Marcus Garvey* (Kingston, Jamaica: Gleaner, 1940), p. 91.

protect the rights of the race. The convention also stressed the need to improve the health of black people and created a U.N.I.A. department of health and public education for this purpose, with special emphasis on the needs of isolated Negro communities. The enthusiasm and dedication of the delegates demonstrated that the Universal Negro Improvement Association was still very much alive and that Marcus Garvey remained a force to be reckoned with, in Jamaica and throughout the black world.

Indeed, for a time it seemed that Garvey might assume a dominant role in Jamaican politics. Before the 1929 convention he had organized the Jamaican Peoples Political Party, which advocated a larger degree of self-government for the island within the British imperial system as well as a comprehensive program of economic and social reforms. He publicized his political views in his daily paper, the *Black Man*, established in March 1929 as the militant champion of the Jamaican black masses. Garvey himself was elected to a seat on the Kingston and St. Andrew Corporation, the governing body for the city of Kingston and its surrounding parish. His campaign in the 1930 elections for a seat in the Jamaican legislature was unsuccessful, however, probably because of the limited Jamaican suffrage and the adverse publicity stemming from a series of legal altercations, one of which led to his serving a three-month sentence for contempt of court. These disputes arose from a growing split between Garvey's current Jamaica-based movement and some of his former associates in the United States. A number of American delegates to the 1929 convention had been offended by Garvey's assertion that the headquarters of the movement was now in Jamaica; they insisted instead that it remain in New York, where the association was incorporated and had enjoyed its greatest growth. Garvey proceeded to incorporate a new Parent Body of the Universal Negro Improvement Association in Jamaica, and with only partial success urged all local divisions to get new charters from the Jamaican headquarters. He soon found himself involved in a number of unexpected lawsuits over debts of the insolvent American association, however, and ultimately the unfortunate schism deprived his Jamaica-based U.N.I.A. of a $300,000 legacy.

The depression years of the 1930s saw the gradual disintegration and decline of the once mighty Garvey movement. Following the demise of his Jamaican newspapers and of the *Negro World* in 1933, Garvey began intermittent publication of a monthly magazine, the *Black Man*, as a means of keeping in contact with his scattered but dwindling legions. His failure to gain a significant foothold in Jamaican politics and the disappointing turnout for the seventh U.N.I.A. convention held in Kingston in 1934 led him to move his headquarters to London the following year. Here he continued with undiminished enthusiasm to appeal for Negro unity and pride in the race's African heritage. But for the most part the black masses were no longer listening or responding; their concern in the depression years was individual survival, not the redemption of Africa or the rehabilitation of the race. Garvey presided over small meetings of the U.N.I.A. in Toronto in 1936, 1937, and 1938, and launched a School of African Philosophy through which he offered direct and correspondence work in black studies, an educational enterprise reminiscent of the U.N.I.A. institute operated for a time at Claremont, Virginia, in the 1920s. Only a handful of students appeared, however, and the decline of his once massive international association was painfully evident.

Twice in the late thirties Garvey was dangerously stricken with pneumonia, for his health had never been robust, and his chronic asthma was aggravated by the damp chill of the English climate. In January of 1940 he suffered a severe stroke which left him badly paralyzed on the right side. He was only fifty-two, so there seemed reason to hope for a recovery; in fact, after a slow convalescence he regained enough strength to take rides in Hyde Park, where he had so often championed Negro rights in the past. Toward the end of May his health began to fail rapidly, however, leading a news service to send out an erroneous report of his death. The notice was only a bit premature, for the end finally and mercifully came on June 10, 1940. In life Garvey had commanded more than passing notice at Whitehall, but now Britons were intent upon the miraculous drama unfolding on the beaches of Dunkirk, and his passing went unnoticed. His death received more attention in the United States, the scene of his greatest triumphs and setbacks, and white and black newspapers alike paid mixed tribute to the memory of the daring little Jamaican who had once dominated the American race scene. They differed widely in their appraisal of his significance, but they agreed on one point: Marcus Garvey's like would not soon be seen again.

Chronology of the Life of Marcus Garvey

1887   Born on August 17 in St. Ann's Bay on the northern coast of Jamaica.

1904   After elementary schooling and apprenticeship, moved to the capital city of Kingston to work as a printer.

1907   Participated in an unsuccessful printers' strike and became interested in reform, though skeptical of the value of trade unions for black workers.

1912–14   Lived and studied in England, where he developed his lifelong interest in Africa.

1914   Returned to Jamaica and established the Universal Negro Improvement Association.

1916   Moved to the United States, seeking expanded support for his black self-help movement.

1918   Began publication of the Negro World, which quickly became a leading American black weekly with circulation throughout the black world.

1919   Established the Black Star Line to link the Negroes of the world.

1920   Presided over the first international convention of the U.N.I.A. in Harlem, demonstrating his impressive mass following.

1922   Indicted with three associates for mail fraud after the Black Star Line went bankrupt, losing its three ships.

1923   Convicted of mail fraud; released on bail pending appeal.

1924   Organized a new maritime venture, the Black Cross Navigation and Trading Company, and acquired another ship; dispatched a mission to Liberia in preparation for an abortive colonization plan.

1925   Conviction upheld; imprisoned in Atlanta penitentiary.

1927   Sentence commuted by President Coolidge; deported to Jamaica.

1928   Toured Europe and petitioned the League of Nations for a redress of Negro grievances, urging the creation of an independent black nation in Africa.

1929   Presided over the revitalized U.N.I.A.'s sixth international convention in Kingston, Jamaica; organized the Jamaican Peoples Political Party.

1930   Elected to a seat on the Kingston municipal council, but defeated for a seat in the Jamaican legislature.

17

1934   Disappointed at meager attendance at the seventh U.N.I.A. convention in Jamaica.

1935   Moved to London for better contact with his scattered and diminished following; began publication of a monthly magazine, the *Black Man.*

1936–38 Presided over small annual meetings of the U.N.I.A. in Toronto; organized a School of African Philosophy.

1940   Suffered a severe stroke and died in London on June 10 at the age of fifty-two.

GARVEY LOOKS AT THE WORLD

A master publicist, Marcus Garvey was equally effective with tongue or pen. For more than a decade after World War I, no other Negro leader even remotely rivaled his ability to reach and inspire the black masses of the Americas and even Africa. Garvey's single-minded dedication to the cause of Negro rights and African redemption led him to produce a veritable torrent of speeches, editorials, essays, manifestoes, and petitions during his comparatively brief life. On occasion his style was introspective and philosophical; more commonly the race's past and future glories were portrayed in vividly persuasive yet simple phrases. Garvey wrote chiefly for his various newspapers and periodicals: the weekly Negro World *and the daily* Negro Times, *launched while he was in New York; the daily* Black Man *and daily* New Jamaican, *which he established after his return to Jamaica in 1927; and the monthly* Black Man, *published irregularly after he moved to London in 1935. His wife, Amy Jacques Garvey, edited a valuable collection of his early writings,* Philosophy and Opinions of Marcus Garvey, *which appeared in two volumes in 1923 and 1926. Long out of print and extremely rare, this work has recently been reprinted in the United States and England. It constitutes the best single source for an understanding of Garvey's ideas and program as well as his remarkable appeal.*

1

From Jamaica to New York[1]

Marcus Garvey's remarkable success as a race leader began only after he moved to the United States in 1916. Two

[1] From Amy Jacques Garvey, ed., *Philosophy and Opinions of Marcus Garvey,* vol. II (New York: Universal Publishing House, 1926), pp. 124–27, 129, 130–31; Marcus Garvey (Kingston) to Booker T. Washington (Tuskegee) April 12, 1915,

*years earlier, upon his return to Jamaica after eighteen months
of study and travel in Europe, he had founded the Universal
Negro Improvement and Conservation Association and African
Communities' League (usually shortened to U.N.I.A). His immediate purpose was to establish an industrial and agricultural
school for poor Jamaican blacks modeled after Booker T. Washington's Tuskegee Institute. Although Washington himself gave
encouragement, the U.N.I.A. at first attracted little interest or
support in Jamaica. To raise funds, Garvey visited the United
States in the spring of 1916 and received such a warm response
that he shifted his headquarters to Harlem. There, for the better
part of the next decade, he dominated the Negro world and
launched a variety of political and economic ventures, including
the ill-fated Black Star Line, whose bankruptcy ultimately led to
his downfall and imprisonment. The following selections review
Garvey's efforts to establish a great international movement for
Negro redemption. The first and third parts are from one of his
rare autobiographical writings, addressed to a white audience
shortly after his conviction for mail fraud in 1923. The middle
selection, his 1915 letter to Booker T. Washington indicating his
intention to visit the United States, includes a copy of the earliest
known manifesto outlining the aims of the new Universal Negro
Improvement Association.*

I was born in the Island of Jamaica, British West Indies, on
August 17, 1887. My parents were black Negroes. My father was a
man of brilliant intellect and dashing courage. He was unafraid of
consequences. He took human chances in the course of life, as most
bold men do, and he failed at the close of his career. He once had a
fortune; he died poor. My mother was a sober and conscientious
Christian, too soft and good for the time in which she lived. She was
the direct opposite of my father. He was severe, firm, determined, bold
and strong, refusing to yield even to superior forces if he believed he
was right. My mother, on the other hand, was always willing to return
a smile for a blow, and ever ready to bestow charity upon her enemy.
Of this strange combination I was born thirty-six years ago, and ushered into a world of sin, the flesh and the devil.

I grew up with other black and white boys. I was never whipped
by any, but made them all respect the strength of my arms. I got my
education from many sources—through private tutors, two public

Booker T. Washington Papers, Library of Congress. Both selections reprinted by
permission of Amy Jacques Garvey.

schools, two grammar or high schools and two colleges. My teachers were men and women of varied experiences and abilities; four of them were eminent preachers. They studied me and I studied them. With some I became friendly in after years; others and I drifted apart, because as a boy they wanted to whip me, and I simply refused to be whipped. I was not made to be whipped. It annoys me to be defeated; hence to me, to be once defeated is to find cause for an everlasting struggle to reach the top.

I became a printer's apprentice at an early age, while still attending school. My apprentice master was a highly educated and alert man. In the affairs of business and the world he had no peer. He taught me many things before I reached twelve, and at fourteen I had enough intelligence and experience to manage men. I was strong and manly, and I made them respect me. I developed a strong and forceful character, and have maintained it still.

To me, at home in my early days, there was no difference between white and black. One of my father's properties, the place where I lived most of the time, was adjoining that of a white man. He had three girls and two boys; the Wesleyan minister, another white man, whose church my parents attended, also had property adjoining ours. He had three girls and one boy. All of us were playmates. We romped and were happy children, playmates together. The little white girl whom I liked most knew no better than I did myself. We were two innocent fools who never dreamed of a race feeling and problem. As a child, I went to school with white boys and girls, like all other Negroes. We were not called Negroes then. I never heard the term Negro used once until I was about fourteen.

At fourteen my little white playmate and I parted. Her parents thought the time had come to separate us and draw the color line. They sent her and another sister to Edinburgh, Scotland, and told her that she was never to write or try to get in touch with me, for I was a "nigger." It was then that I found for the first time that there was some difference in humanity, and that there were different races, each having its own separate and distinct social life. I did not care about the separation after I was told about it, because I never thought all during our childhood association that the girl and the rest of the children of her race were better than I was; in fact, they used to look up to me. So I simply had no regrets.

After my first lesson in race distinction, I never thought of playing with white girls any more, even if they might be next-door neighbors. At home my sisters' company was good enough for me, and at school I made friends with the colored girls next to me. White boys and I used to frolic together. We played cricket and baseball, ran races and rode bicycles together, took each other to the river and to the sea

beach to learn to swim, and made boyish efforts while out in deep
water to drown each other, making a sprint for shore crying out
"Shark, shark, shark!" In all our experiences, however, only one black
boy was drowned. He went under on a Friday afternoon after school
hours, and his parents found him afloat, half eaten by sharks, on
the following Sunday afternoon. Since then we boys never went sea
bathing.

At maturity the black and white boys separated, and took different
courses in life. I grew then to see the difference between the races more
and more. My schoolmates as young men did not know or remember
me any more. Then I realized that I had to make a fight for a place
in the world, that it was not so easy to pass on to office and position.
Personally, however, I had not much difficulty in finding and holding
a place for myself, for I was aggressive. At eighteen I had an excellent
position as manager of a large printing establishment, having under
my control several men old enough to be my grandfathers. But I got
mixed up with public life. I started to take an interest in the politics
of my country, and then I saw the injustice done to my race because
it was black, and I became dissatisfied on that account. I went traveling to South and Central America and parts of the West Indies to
find out if it was so elsewhere, and I found the same situation. I set
sail for Europe to find out if it was different there, and again I found
the stumbling block—"You are black." I read of the conditions in
America. I read "Up from Slavery," by Booker T. Washington, and
then my doom—if I may so call it—of being a race leader dawned
upon me in London after I had traveled through almost half of Europe.

I asked: "Where is the black man's Government?" "Where is his
King and his kingdom?" "Where is his President, his country, and
his ambassador, his army, his navy, his men of big affairs?" I could
not find them, and then I declared, "I will help to make them."

Becoming naturally restless for the opportunity of doing something
for the advancement of my race, I was determined that the black man
would not continue to be kicked about by all the other races and
nations of the world, as I saw it in the West Indies, South and Central
America and Europe, and as I read of it in America. My young and
ambitious mind led me into flights of great imagination. I saw before
me then, even as I do now, a new world of black men, not peons, serfs,
dogs and slaves, but a nation of sturdy men making their impress upon
civilization and causing a new light to dawn upon the human race. I
could not remain in London any more. My brain was afire. There was
a world of thought to conquer. I had to start ere it became too late and
the work be not done. Immediately I boarded a ship at Southampton
for Jamaica, where I arrived on July 15, 1914. The Universal Negro

Improvement Association and African Communities (Imperial) League was founded and organized five days after my arrival, with the program of uniting all the Negro peoples of the world into one great body to establish a country and Government absolutely their own.

Where did the name of the organization come from? It was while speaking to a West Indian Negro who was a passenger on the ship with me from Southampton, who was returning home to the West Indies from Basutoland with his Basuto wife, that I further learned of the horrors of native life in Africa. He related to me such horrible and pitiable tales that my heart bled within me. Retiring to my cabin, all day and the following night I pondered over the subject matter of that conversation, and at midnight, lying flat on my back, the vision and thought came to me that I should name the organization the Universal Negro Improvement Association and African Communities (Imperial) League. Such a name I thought would embrace the purpose of all black humanity. Thus to the world a name was born, a movement created, and a man became known.

LETTER TO DR. BOOKER T. WASHINGTON: APRIL 12, 1915

Dear Doctor Washington:

Some time last year I wrote to you informing you of my proposed visit to America to lecture in the interest of my Association and you were good enough to write to me inviting me to see your great institution.

I am expecting to leave for America between May and June and I shall be calling on you. I intend to do most of my public speaking in the South among the people of our race. I enclose you a manifesto of our Association which will give you an idea of the objects we have in view. I am now asking you to do your best to assist me during my stay in America, as I shall be coming there a stranger to the people.

I need not reacquaint you of the horrible conditions prevailing among our people in the West Indies as you are so well informed of happenings all over Negrodom.

Trusting to be favored with an early reply.

P.S. I take the opportunity of enclosing you patron's tickets for our concert to which we ask you patronage, as also envelope.

Manifesto of the Universal Negro Improvement Association

THE UNIVERSAL
NEGRO IMPROVEMENT AND CONSERVATION ASSOCIATION
AND AFRICAN COMMUNITIES' LEAGUE

FOUNDED AUGUST 1, 1914.

In view of the universal disunity existing among the people of the Negro or African race, and the apparent danger which must follow the continuance of such a spirit, it has been deemed fit and opportune to found a Society with a universal programme, for the purpose of drawing the peoples of the race together, hence the organization above-named.

All people of Negro or African parentage are requested to join in with us for the propagation and achievement of the following objects.

GENERAL OBJECTS:

To establish a Universal Confraternity among the race.
To promote the spirit of race pride and love.
To reclaim the fallen of the race.
To administer to and assist the needy.
To assist in civilizing the backward tribes of Africa.
To strengthen the imperialism of independent African States.
To establish Commissionaries or Agencies in the principal countries of the world for the protection of all Negroes, irrespective of nationality.
To promote a conscientious Christian worship among the native tribes of Africa.
To establish Universities, Colleges and Secondary Schools for the further education and culture of the boys and girls of the race.
To conduct a world-wide commercial and industrial intercourse.

LOCAL (JAMAICA) OBJECTS:

To establish educational and industrial colleges for the further education and culture of our boys and girls.
To reclaim the fallen and degraded (especially the criminal class) and help them to a state of good citizenship.
To administer to, and assist the needy.
To promote a better taste for commerce and industry.
To promote a universal confraternity and strengthen the bonds of brotherhood and unity among the races.
To help generally in the development of the country.

> MARCUS GARVEY, *President and Travelling Commissioner.*
> THOS. SMIKLE, *Vice-President.*
> EVA ALDRED, *President Ladies' Division.*
> T. A. MC CORMACK, *General Secretary.*
> *Office:* 30 CHARLES STREET, KINGSTON, JAMAICA.

BOARD OF MANAGEMENT.

Marcus Garvey, Thomas Smikle, T. A. McCormack, Adrian A. Daily, E. E. Reid, T. T. Brown, J. R. Murdock, A. Peart, Arthur McKenzie, J. M. Reid, A. Knight,

Robert Cross, Eva Aldred, Amy Ashwood, Gwen. Campbell, Connie Phillips, Mrs. A. Peart and Amy Aldred.

APPLICATION FOR MEMBERSHIP.

Secretary Universal Negro Improvement Association,
    30 Charles Street, Kingston.

Dear Sir,
    Please register me as an active member of our Society and send me from time to time all literature published by you. I enclose sixpence 6d. as my first monthly due.

Name..

Profession.....................................

Address..

The organization under my Presidency grew by leaps and bounds. I started The Negro World. Being a journalist, I edited this paper free of cost for the Association, and worked for them without pay until November, 1920. I traveled all over the country for the Association at my own expense and established branches until in 1919 we had about thirty branches in different cities. By my writings and speeches we were able to build up a large organization of over 2,000,000 by June, 1919, at which time we launched the program of the Black Star Line. . . .

The first year of our activities for the Black Star Line added prestige to the Universal Negro Improvement Association. Several hundred thousand dollars worth of shares were sold. Our first ship, the steamship Yarmouth, had made three voyages to the West Indies and Central America. The white press had flashed the news all over the world. I, a young Negro, as President of the corporation, had become famous. My name was discussed on five continents. The Universal Negro Improvement Association gained millions of followers all over the world. By August, 1920, over 4,000,000 persons had joined the movement. A convention of all the Negro peoples of the world was called to meet in New York that month. Delegates came from all parts of the known world. Over 25,000 persons packed the Madison Square Garden on August 1 to hear me speak to the first International Convention of Negroes. It was a record breaking meeting, the first and the biggest of its kind. The name of Garvey had become known as a leader of his race.

Such fame among Negroes was too much for other race leaders and politicians to tolerate. My downfall was planned by my enemies. They laid all kinds of traps for me. They scattered their spies among the employes of the Black Star Line and the Universal Negro Improvement Association. Our office records were stolen. Employes started to be openly dishonest; we could get no convictions against them; even if on complaint they were held by a Magistrate, they were dismissed by the Grand Jury. The ships' officers started to pile up thousands of dollars of debts against the company without the knowledge of the officers of the corporation. Our ships were damaged at sea, and there was a general riot of wreck and ruin. Officers of the Universal Negro Improvement Association also began to steal and be openly dishonest. I had to dismiss them. They joined my enemies, and thus I had an endless fight on my hands to save the ideals of the Association and carry out our program for the race. My Negro enemies, finding that they alone could not destroy me, resorted to misrepresenting me to the leaders of the white race, several of whom, without proper investigation, also opposed me.

With robberies from within and from without, the Black Star Line was forced to suspend active business in December, 1921. While I was on a business trip to the West Indies in the Spring of 1921, the Black Star Line received the blow from which it was unable to recover. A sum of $25,000 was paid by one of the officers of the corporation to a man to purchase a ship, but the ship was never obtained and the money was never returned. The company was defrauded of a further sum of $11,000. Through such actions on the part of dishonest men in the shipping business, the Black Star Line received its first setback. This resulted in my being indicted for using the United States mails to defraud investors in the company. I was subsequently convicted and sentenced to five years in a Federal penitentiary. My trial is a matter of history. I know I was not given a square deal, because my indictment was the result of a "frame-up" among my political and business enemies. I had to conduct my own case in court because of the peculiar position in which I found myself. I had millions of friends and a large number of enemies. I wanted a colored attorney to handle my case, but there was none I could trust. I feel that I have been denied justice because of prejudice. Yet I have an abundance of faith in the courts of America, and I hope yet to obtain justice on my appeal.

The temporary ruin of the Black Star Line has in no way affected the larger work of the Universal Negro Improvement Association, which now has 900 branches with an approximate membership of 6,000,000. This organization has succeeded in organizing the Negroes all over the world, and we now look forward to a renaissance that will create a new people and bring about the restoration of Ethiopia's ancient glory.

2
Garvey Maxims[1]

Although he attracted the support of some Negro intellectuals and businessmen, Garvey's real strength lay with the downtrodden black masses, who responded enthusiastically to his bold call to unite scattered Africa for the redemption of the motherland. No doubt part of Garvey's unmatched success with the masses derived from his ability to coin stirring slogans like the U.N.I.A. motto: "One Aim! One God! One Destiny!" Often his imagery was dramatic, his style almost poetic; always he championed Negro pride. The following Garvey maxims are representative of the collection published by his wife in 1923.

What you do to-day that is worthwhile, inspires others to act at some future time.

There is nothing in the world common to man, that man cannot do.

The ends you serve that are selfish will take you no further than yourself; but the ends you serve that are for all, in common, will take you even into eternity.

EDUCATION is the medium by which a people are prepared for the creation of their own particular civilization, and the advancement and glory of their own race.

The masses make the nation and the race. If the masses are illiterate, that is the judgment passed on the race by those who are critical of its existence.

Every student of Political Science, every student of Economics knows, that the race can only be saved through a solid industrial foundation. That the race can only be saved through political independence. Take

[1] From Amy Jacques Garvey, ed., *Philosophy and Opinions of Marcus Garvey*, vol. I (New York: Universal Publishing House, 1923), pp. 1, 2, 4, 5, 6, 7, 8, 9, 10, 13. Reprinted by permission of Amy Jacques Garvey.

*away industry from a race; take away political freedom from a race, and
you have a group of slaves.*

*Be as proud of your race today as our fathers were in days of yore.
We have beautiful history, and we shall create another in the future
that will astonish the world.*

*So many of us find excuses to get out of the Negro Race, because we
are led to believe that the race is unworthy—that it has not accomplished anything. Cowards that we are! It is we who are unworthy, because we are not contributing to the uplift and upbuilding of this
noble race.*

*For over three hundred years the white man has been our oppressor,
and he naturally is not going to liberate us to the higher freedom—
the truer liberty—the truer Democracy. We have to liberate ourselves.*

*Let us prepare TODAY. For the TOMORROWS in the lives of the
nations will be so eventful that Negroes everywhere will be called upon
to play their part in the survival of the fittest human group.*

*The evolutionary scale that weighs nations and races, balances alike
for peoples; hence we feel sure that some day the balance will register
a change for the Negro.*

*The world ought to know that it could not keep 400,000,000 Negroes
down forever.*

*There is always a turning point in the destiny of every race, every
nation, of all peoples, and we have come now to the turning point of
Negro, where we have changed from the old cringing weakling, and
transformed into full-grown men, demanding our portion as MEN.*

A race without authority and power, is a race without respect.

*The only protection against INJUSTICE in man is POWER—Physi-
cal, financial and scientific.*

Men who are in earnest are not afraid of consequences.

CHANCE has never yet satisfied the hope of a suffering people.

*Action, self-reliance, the vision of self and the future have been the
only means by which the oppressed have seen and realized the light of
their own freedom.*

Any sane man, race or nation that desires freedom must first of all think in terms of blood. Why even the Heavenly Father tells us that "without the shedding of blood there can be no remission of sins." Then how in the name of God, with history before us, do we expect to redeem Africa without preparing ourselves—some of us to die.

LEADERSHIP means everything—PAIN, BLOOD, DEATH.

Let Africa be our guiding Star—OUR STAR OF DESTINY.

How dare anyone tell us that Africa cannot be redeemed, when we have 400,000,000 men and women with warm blood coursing through their veins?

The power that holds Africa is not Divine. The power that holds Africa is human, and it is recognized that whatsoever man has done, man can do.

All of us may not live to see the higher accomplishment of an African Empire—so strong and powerful, as to compel the respect of mankind, but we in our life-time can so work and act as to make the dream a possibility within another generation.

Wake up Ethiopia! Wake up Africa! Let us work towards the one glorious end of a free, redeemed and mighty nation. Let Africa be a bright star among the constellation of nations.

No one knows when the hour of Africa's Redemption cometh. It is in the wind. It is coming. One day, like a storm, it will be here. When that day comes all Africa will stand together.

3

Declaration of Rights of the Negro Peoples of the World[1]

Perhaps the high point of the Garvey movement was the first international convention of the U.N.I.A., which took place in New York during August of 1920. Delegates came from every part of the United States and a score of foreign countries including Africa. The gathering, a virtual black League of Nations, was a stunning triumph for its leader. The convention elected Garvey the Provisional President of Africa, leader of a kind of government-in-exile, and drafted a Declaration of Rights detailing the grievances and demands of Negroes everywhere. The document contained the most comprehensive and explicit program Garvey ever offered and probably reflcted the diversity of interests represented among the delegates at this largest of Garvey conventions. As the Black Star Line and other ventures failed, Garvey increasingly stressed race pride and purity, and especially African redemption, issues which he undoubtedly recognized as less controversial in the eyes of white Americans than the Declaration's explicit denunciation of discrimination and unequal treatment.

Preamble

"Be it Resolved, That the Negro people of the world, through their chosen representatives in convention assembled in Liberty Hall, in the City of New York and United States of America, from August 1 to August 31, in the year of our Lord, one thousand nine hundred and twenty, protest against the wrongs and injustices they are suffering at the hands of their white brethren, and state what they deem their fair and just rights, as well as the treatment they propose to demand of all men in the future."

We complain:

[1] From Amy Jacques Garvey, ed., *Philosophy and Opinions of Marcus Garvey*, vol. II (New York: Universal Publishing House, 1926), pp. 135–42. Reprinted by permission of Amy Jacques Garvey.

I. "That nowhere in the world, with few exceptions, are black men accorded equal treatment with white men, although in the same situation and circumstances, but, on the contrary, are discriminated against and denied the common rights due to human beings for no other reason than their race and color."

"We are not willingly accepted as guests in the public hotels and inns of the world for no other reason than our race and color."

II. "In certain parts of the United States of America our race is denied the right of public trial accorded to other races when accused of crime, but are lynched and burned by mobs, and such brutal and inhuman treatment is even practised upon our women."

III. "That European nations have parcelled out among themselves and taken possession of nearly all of the continent of Africa, and the natives are compelled to surrender their lands to aliens and are treated in most instances like slaves."

IV. "In the southern portion of the United States of America, although citizens under the Federal Constitution, and in some states almost equal to the whites in population and are qualified land owners and taxpayers, we are, nevertheless, denied all voice in the making and administration of the laws and are taxed without representation by the state governments, and at the same time compelled to do military service in defense of the country."

V. "On the public conveyances and common carriers in the Southern portion of the United States we are jim-crowed and compelled to accept separate and inferior accommodations and made to pay the same fare charged for first-class accommodations, and our families are often humiliated and insulted by drunken white men who habitually pass through the jim-crow cars going to the smoking car."

VI. "The physicians of our race are denied the right to attend their patients while in the public hospitals of the cities and states where they reside in certain parts of the United States."

"Our children are forced to attend inferior separate schools for shorter terms than white children, and the public school funds are unequally divided between the white and colored schools."

VII. "We are discriminated against and denied an equal chance to earn wages for the support of our families, and in many instances are refused admission into labor unions, and nearly everywhere are paid smaller wages than white men."

VIII. "In Civil Service and departmental offices we are everywhere discriminated against and made to feel that to be a black man in Europe, America and the West Indies is equivalent to being an outcast and a leper among the races of men, no matter what the character and attainments of the black man may be."

IX. "In the British and other West Indian Islands and colonies,

Negroes are secretly and cunningly discriminated against, and denied those fuller rights in government to which white citizens are appointed, nominated and elected."

X. "That our people in those parts are forced to work for lower wages than the average standard of white men and are kept in conditions repugnant to good civilized tastes and customs."

XI. "That the many acts of injustice against members of our race before the courts of law in the respective islands and colonies are of such nature as to create disgust and disrespect for the white man's sense of justice."

XII. "Against all such inhuman, unchristian and uncivilized treatment we here and now emphatically protest, and invoke the condemnation of all mankind."

"In order to encourage our race all over the world and to stimulate it to a higher and grander destiny, we demand and insist on the following Declaration of Rights:

1. "Be it known to all men that whereas, all men are created equal and entitled to the rights of life, liberty and the pursuit of happiness, and because of this we, the duly elected representatives of the Negro peoples of the world, invoking the aid of the just and Almighty God do declare all men women and children of our blood throughout the world free citizens, and do claim them as free citizens of Africa, the Motherland of all Negroes."

2. "That we believe in the supreme authority of our race in all things racial; that all things are created and given to man as a common possession; that there should be an equitable distribution and apportionment of all such things, and in consideration of the fact that as a race we are now deprived of those things that are morally and legally ours, we believe it right that all such things should be acquired and held by whatsoever means possible."

3. "That we believe the Negro, like any other race, should be governed by the ethics of civilization, and, therefore, should not be deprived of any of those rights or privileges common to other human beings."

4. "We declare that Negroes, wheresoever they form a community among themselves, should be given the right to elect their own representatives to represent them in legislatures, courts of law, or such institutions as may exercise control over that particular community."

5. "We assert that the Negro is entitled to even-handed justice before all courts of law and equity in whatever country he may be found, and when this is denied him on account of his race or color such denial is an insult to the race as a whole and should be resented by the entire body of Negroes."

6. "We declare it unfair and prejudicial to the rights of Negroes in

communities where they exist in considerable numbers to be tried by a judge and jury composed entirely of an alien race, but in all such cases members of our race are entitled to representation on the jury."

7. "We believe that any law or practice that tends to deprive any African of his land or the privileges of free citizenship within his country is unjust and immoral, and no native should respect any such law or practice."

8. "We declare taxation without representation unjust and tyrannous, and there should be no obligation on the part of the Negro to obey the levy of a tax by any law-making body from which he is excluded and denied representation on account of his race and color."

9. "We believe that any law especially directed against the Negro to his detriment and singling him out because of his race or color is unfair and immoral, and should not be respected."

10. "We believe all men entitled to common human respect, and that our race should in no way tolerate any insults that may be interpreted to mean disrespect to our color."

11. "We deprecate the use of the term 'nigger' as applied to Negroes, and demand that the word 'Negro' be written with a capital 'N.' "

12. "We believe that the Negro should adopt every means to protect himself against barbarous practices inflicted upon him because of color."

13. "We believe in the freedom of Africa for the Negro people of the world, and by the principle of Europe for the Europeans and Asia for the Asiatics; we also demand Africa for the Africans at home and abroad."

14. "We believe in the inherent right of the Negro to possess himself of Africa, and that his possession of same shall not be regarded as an infringement on any claim or purchase made by any race or nation."

15. "We strongly condemn the cupidity of those nations of the world who, by open aggression or secret schemes, have seized the territories and inexhaustible natural wealth of Africa, and we place on record our most solemn determination to reclaim the treasures and possession of the vast continent of our forefathers."

16. "We believe all men should live in peace one with the other, but when races and nations provoke the ire of other races and nations by attempting to infringe upon their rights, war becomes inevitable, and the attempt in any way to free one's self or protect one's rights or heritage becomes justifiable."

17. "Whereas, the lynching, by burning, hanging or any other means, of human beings is a barbarous practice, and a shame and disgrace to civilization, we therefore declare any country guilty of such atrocities outside the pale of civilization."

18. "We protest against the atrocious crime of whipping, flogging and overworking of the native tribes of Africa and Negroes everywhere. These are methods that should be abolished, and all means should be taken to prevent a continuance of such brutal practices."

19. "We protest against the atrocious practice of shaving the heads of Africans, especially of African women or individuals of Negro blood, when placed in prison as a punishment for crime by an alien race."

20. "We protest against segregated districts, separate public conveyances, industrial discrimination, lynchings and limitations of political privileges of any Negro citizen in any part of the world on account of race, color or creed, and will exert our full influence and power against all such."

21. "We protest against any punishment inflicted upon a Negro with severity, as against lighter punishment inflicted upon another of an alien race for like offense, as an act of prejudice and injustice, and should be resented by the entire race."

22. "We protest against the system of education in any country where Negroes are denied the same privileges and advantages as other races."

23. "We declare it inhuman and unfair to boycott Negroes from industries and labor in any part of the world."

24. "We believe in the doctrine of the freedom of the press, and we therefore emphatically protest against the suppression of Negro newspapers and periodicals in various parts of the world, and call upon Negroes everywhere to employ all available means to prevent such suppression."

25. "We further demand free speech universally for all men."

26. "We hereby protest against the publication of scandalous and inflammatory articles by an alien press tending to create racial strife and the exhibition of picture films showing the Negro as a cannibal."

27. "We believe in the self-determination of all peoples."

28. "We declare for the freedom of religious worship."

29. "With the help of Almighty God, we declare ourselves the sworn protectors of the honor and virtue of our women and children, and pledge our lives for their protection and defense everywhere, and under all circumstances from wrongs and outrages."

30. "We demand the right of unlimited and unprejudiced education for ourselves and our posterity forever."

31. "We declare that the teaching in any school by alien teachers to our boys and girls, that the alien race is superior to the Negro race, is an insult to the Negro people of the world."

32. "Where Negroes form a part of the citizenry of any country, and pass the civil service examination of such country, we declare them

entitled to the same consideration as other citizens as to appointments in such civil service."

33. "We vigorously protest against the increasingly unfair and unjust treatment accorded Negro travelers on land and sea by the agents and employees of railroad and steamship companies and insist that for equal fare we receive equal privileges with travelers of other races."

34. "We declare it unjust for any country, State or nation to enact laws tending to hinder and obstruct the free immigration of Negroes on account of their race and color."

35. "That the right of the Negro to travel unmolested throughout the world be not abridged by any person or persons, and all Negroes are called upon to give aid to a fellow Negro when thus molested."

36. "We declare that all Negroes are entitled to the same right to travel over the world as other men."

37. "We hereby demand that the governments of the world recognize our leader and his representatives chosen by the race to look after the welfare of our people under such governments."

38. "We demand complete control of our social institutions without interference by any alien race or races."

39. "That the colors, Red, Black and Green, be the colors of the Negro race."

40. "Resolved, That the anthem 'Ethiopia, Thou Land of Our Fathers,' etc., shall be the anthem of the Negro race."

The Universal Ethiopian Anthem
by Burrell and Ford

I

Ethiopia, thou land of our fathers,
Thou land where the gods loved to be,
As storm cloud at night suddenly gathers
Our armies come rushing to thee.
We must in the fight be victorious
When swords are thrust outward to gleam;
For us will the vict'ry be glorious
When led by the red, black and green.

Chorus

Advance, advance to victory,
Let Africa be free;
Advance to meet the foe
With the might
Of the red, the black and the green.

II

Ethiopia, the tyrant's falling,
Who smote thee upon thy knees,
And thy children are lustily calling
From over the distant seas.
Jehovah, the Great One has heard us,
Has noted our sighs and our tears,
With His spirit of Love he has stirred us
To be One through the coming years.

Chorus

Advance, advance, etc.

III

O Jehovah, thou God of the ages
Grant unto our sons that lead
The wisdom Thou gave to Thy sages
When Israel was sore in need.
Thy voice thro' the dim past has spoken,
Ethiopia shall stretch forth her hand,
By Thee shall all fetters be broken,
And Heav'n bless our dear fatherland.

Chorus

Advance, advance, etc.

41. "We believe that any limited liberty which deprives one of the complete rights and prerogatives of full citizenship is but a modified form of slavery."

42. "We declare it an injustice to our people and a serious impediment to the health of the race to deny to competent licensed Negro physicians the right to practise in the public hospitals of the communities in which they reside, for no other reason than their race and color."

43. "We call upon the various governments of the world to accept and acknowledge Negro representatives who shall be sent to the said governments to represent the general welfare of the Negro peoples of the world."

44. "We deplore and protest against the practice of confining juvenile prisoners in prisons with adults, and we recommend that such youthful prisoners be taught gainful trades under humane supervision."

45. "Be it further resolved, that we as a race of people declare the

League of Nations null and void as far as the Negro is concerned, in that it seeks to deprive Negroes of their liberty."

46. "We demand of all men to do unto us as we would do unto them, in the name of justice; and we cheerfully accord to all men all the rights we claim herein for ourselves."

47. "We declare that no Negro shall engage himself in battle for an alien race without first obtaining the consent of the leader of the Negro people of the world, except in a matter of national self-defense."

48. "We protest against the practice of drafting Negroes and sending them to war with alien forces without proper training, and demand in all cases that Negro soldiers be given the same training as the aliens."

49. "We demand that instructions given Negro children in schools include the subject of 'Negro History,' to their benefit."

50. "We demand a free and unfettered commercial intercourse with all the Negro people of the world."

51. "We declare for the absolute freedom of the seas for all peoples."

52. "We demand that our duly accredited representatives be given proper recognition in all leagues, conferences, conventions or courts of international arbitration wherever human rights are discussed."

53. "We proclaim the 31st day of August of each year to be an international holiday to be observed by all Negroes."

54. "We want all men to know we shall maintain and contend for the freedom and equality of every man, woman and child of our race, with our lives, our fortunes and our sacred honor."

These rights we believe to be justly ours and proper for the protection of the Negro race at large, and because of this belief we, on behalf of the four hundred million Negroes of the world, do pledge herein the sacred blood of the race in defense, and we hereby subscribe our names as a guarantee of the truthfulness and faithfulness hereof in the presence of Almighty God, on the 13th day of August, in the year of our Lord one thousand nine hundred and twenty.

4
Building Race Pride[1]

In his speeches, editorials, and even his poetry, Garvey constantly reminded his followers that, whatever their present troubles, they were the descendants of a mighty race whose past glories promised future greatness once the Negroes of the world united to achieve a common destiny. He urged Negroes to think and act black—to be proud of their black skin and distinctively negroid features, to know their honorable history and admire their black heroes, even to worship a black God and a black Christ. This bolstering of the Negro self-image, battered by generations of brutal mistreatment under slavery and imperfect freedom, proved to be Garvey's most enduring legacy and left an indelible mark upon the Negro world.

HISTORY AND THE NEGRO

To read the histories of the world, peoples and races, written by white men, would make the Negro feel and believe that he never amounted to anything in the creation.

History is written with prejudices, likes and dislikes; and there has never been a white historian who ever wrote with any true love or feeling for the Negro.

The Negro should expect but very little by way of compliment from the pen of other races. We are satisfied to know, however, that our race gave the first great civilization to the world; and, for centuries Africa, our ancestral home, was the seat of learning; and when blackmen, who were only fit then for the company of the gods, were philosophers, artists, scientists and men of vision and leadership, the people of other races were groping in savagery, darkness and continental barbarism.

White historians and writers have tried to rob the black man of his proud past in history, and when anything new is discovered to

[1] From Amy Jacques Garvey, ed., *Philosophy and Opinions of Marcus Garvey*, vol. I (New York: Universal Publishing House, 1923), pp. 16, 21–22, 29–30, 33–34; vol. II (New York: Universal Publishing House, 1926), pp. 62, 82–83. Reprinted by permission of Amy Jacques Garvey.

support the race's claim and attest the truthfulness of our greatness in other ages, then it is skillfully rearranged and credited to some other unknown race or people.

Negroes, teach your children that they are direct descendants of the greatest and proudest race who ever peopled the earth; and it is because of the fear of our return to power, in a civilization of our own, that may outshine others, why we are hated and kept down by a jealous and prejudiced contemporary world.

The very fact that the other races will not give the Negro a fair chance is indisputable evidence and proof positive that they are afraid of our civilized progression.

Every falsehood that is told by the historian should be unearthed, and the Negro should not fail to take credit for the glorious and wonderful achievements of his fathers in Africa, Europe and Asia.

Black men were so powerful in the earlier days of history that they were able to impress their civilization, culture and racial characteristics and features upon the peoples of Asia and Southern Europe. The dark Spaniards, Italians and Asiatics are the colored offsprings of a powerful black African civilization and nationalism. Any other statement by historians to the contrary is "bunk" and should not be swallowed by the enlightened Negro.

When we speak of 400,000,000 Negroes we mean to include several of the millions of India who are direct offsprings of that ancient African stock that once invaded Asia. The 400,000,000 Negroes of the world have a beautiful history of their own, and no one of any other race can truly write it but themselves. Until it is completely and carefully written, for the guidance of our children and ourselves, let us think it.

The white man's history is his inspiration, and he should be untrue to himself and negligent of the rights of his posterity to subordinate it to others, and so also of the Negro. Our history is as good as that of any other race or people, and nothing on this side of Heaven or Hell will make us deny it, the false treaties, essays, speculations and philosophies of others notwithstanding.

MISCEGENATION

Some of the men of the Negro race aggravate the race question because they force the white man to conclude that to educate a black man, to give him opportunities, is but to fit him to be a competitor for the hand of his woman; hence the eternal race question.

But not all black men are willing to commit race suicide and to abhor their race for the companionship of another. There are hundreds of millions of us black men who are proud of our skins and to

us the African Empire will not be a Utopia, neither will it be dangerous nor fail to serve our best interests, because we realize that like the
leopard we cannot change our skins.

The men of the highest morals, highest character and noblest pride
are to be found among the masses of the Negro race who love their
women with as much devotion as white men love theirs.

PURITY OF RACE

I believe in a pure black race just as how all self-respecting whites
believe in a pure white race, as far as that can be.

I am conscious of the fact that slavery brought upon us the curse
of many colors within the Negro race, but that is no reason why we
of ourselves should perpetuate the evil; hence instead of encouraging
a wholesale bastardy in the race, we feel that we should now set out
to create a race type and standard of our own which could not, in the
future, be stigmatized by bastardy, but could be recognized and respected as the true race type anteceding even our own time.

RACE ASSIMILATION

Some Negro leaders have advanced the belief that in another few
years the white people will make up their minds to assimilate their
black populations; thereby sinking all racial prejudice in the wel-
coming of the black race into the social companionship of the white.
Such leaders further believe that by the amalgamation of black and
white, a new type will spring up, and that type will become the American and West Indian of the future.

This belief is preposterous. I believe that white men should be
white, yellow men should be yellow, and black men should be black
in the great panorama of races, until each and every race by its own
initiative lifts itself up to the common standard of humanity, as to
compel the respect and appreciation of all, and so make it possible
for each one to stretch out the hand of welcome without being able
to be prejudiced against the other because of any inferior and unfortunate condition.

The white man of America will not, to any organized extent, assimilate the Negro, because in so doing, he feels that he will be com-
mitting racial suicide. This he is not prepared to do. It is true he
illegitimately carries on a system of assimilation; but such assimilation,
as practised, is one that he is not prepared to support because he
becomes prejudiced against his own offspring, if that offspring is the
product of black and white; hence, to the white man the question of
racial differences is eternal. So long as Negroes occupy an inferior

position among the races and nations of the world, just so long will others be prejudiced against them, because it will be profitable for them to keep up their system of superiority. But when the Negro by his own initiative lifts himself from his low state to the highest human standard he will be in a position to stop begging and praying, and demand a place that no individual, race or nation will be able to deny him.

RACE PURITY A DESIDERATUM

It is the duty of the virtuous and morally pure of both the white and black races to thoughtfully and actively protect the future of the two peoples, by vigorously opposing the destructive propaganda and vile efforts of the miscegenationists of the white race, and their associates, the hybrids of the Negro race.

Miscegenation will lead to the moral destruction of both races, and the promotion of a hybrid caste that will have no social standing or moral background in a critical moral judgment of the life and affairs of the human race.

The lower animals, some of even similar but opposite species, do not mate, living voluntarily in keeping with the laws of nature; yet man, the highest type of creation, has to be restrained, in some cases by severe human laws and punishment, from mating with even other species of the lower animals. Something is wrong.

The agitation about and for social equality is but a sham, and all self-respecting whites and blacks should frown upon the extraneous arguments adduced by its advocates.

The Black race, like the white, is proud of its own society and will yield nothing in the desire to keep itself pure and ward off a monstrous subjugation of its original and natural type, by which creation is to be judged, as a race responsible for its own acts, and held accountable in the final analysis for the presentation of itself, before the Judgment seat of God. The Ethiopian cannot change his skin; and we shall not.

THE IMAGE OF GOD

If the white man has the idea of a white God, let him worship his God as he desires. If the yellow man's God is of his race let him worship his God as he sees fit. We, as Negroes, have found a new ideal. Whilst our God has no color, yet it is human to see everything through one's own spectacles, and since the white people have seen their God through white spectacles, we have only now started out (late though it be) to see our God through our own spectacles. The God of Isaac and the God of Jacob let Him exist for the race that believes in the

God of Isaac and the God of Jacob. We Negroes believe in the God of Ethiopia, the everlasting God—God the Father, God the Son and God the Holy Ghost, the One God of all ages. That is the God in whom we believe, but we shall worship Him through the spectacles of Ethiopia.

5

For a New Negro Press[1]

Garvey was sharply critical of the often low journalistic standards of the Negro press in the United States. He believed that most Negro editors, like the bulk of the black clergy, were more concerned with securing their own personal welfare in a white-dominated society than in promoting the interests of their race. The press, he argued, should build the racial pride and unity of its readers by a constructive news and editorial policy. Garvey particularly deplored the extensive advertising carried by Negro newspapers for such products as skin-whiteners and hair-straighteners, which he found degrading to the race. His Negro World *refused such advertising. Such outspoken criticism, as well as Garvey's rejection of the prevailing integrationist philosophy, earned him the enmity of a number of influential Negro editors. Perhaps the most important of these was Robert S. Abbott, whose widely-circulated* Chicago Defender *began attacking Garvey as early as 1919.*

THE "COLORED" OR NEGRO PRESS

The "Colored" or Negro press is the most venal, ignorant and corrupt of our time. This is a broad statement to make against an entire institution, and one so essential to the educational and corporate life of a people; but to be honest and to undeceive the Negro, whom I love above all God's creatures, the truth must be told. I make and again emphasize the statement without any regard for friendship, and with the full knowledge that the said false, vicious and venal press will unmercifully criticise me for telling the truth to the unfortunate of my race.

Unfortunately, the "Colored" or Negro press of today falls into the hands of unprincipled, unscrupulous and characterless individuals whose highest aims are to enrich themselves and to find political berths for themselves and their friends, or, rather, confederates.

[1] From Amy Jacques Garvey, ed., *Philosophy and Opinions of Marcus Garvey,* vol. II (New York: Universal Publishing House, 1926), pp. 77–80. Reprinted by permission of Amy Jacques Garvey.

The white press of today has its element of venality and corruption, but the higher ethics of the profession are generally observed and maintained, and at no time will you find the influence of white journalism used to debase or humiliate its race, but always to promote the highest ideals and protect the integrity of the white people everywhere.

The Negro press, to the contrary, has no constructive policy nor ideal. You may purchase its policy and destroy or kill any professed ideal if you would make the offer in cash.

Negro newspapers will publish the gravest falsehoods without making any effort to first find out the authenticity; they publish the worst crimes and libels against the race, if it pays in circulation or advertisements. A fair example of the criminality of the Negro press against the race is reflected through its most widely circulated sensational publications, namely, "The Chicago Defender" of Chicago, and "The Afro-American" of Baltimore. These newspapers lead all others in their feature of crime, false news and libels against the race.

The primary motive of Negro newspaper promoters is to make quick and easy money. Several of such promoters are alleged to have made large fortunes through their publications, especially through corrupt politics and bad advertisements that should have been refused in respect for the race.

It is plain to see, and is well known, that the sole and only purpose of these promoters is to make money—with absolutely no race pride or effort to help the race toward a proper moral, cultural and educational growth, that would place the race in the category so much desired by the masses and those honest leaders and reformers who have been laboring for the higher development of the people.

To attempt reform or the higher leadership that would permanently benefit the race, is to court the most vicious and cowardly attack from the promoters of Negro newspapers. If you are not in a "ring" with them to support their newspapers or "split" with them, what they would term the "spoils" then you become marked for their crucifixion. All the Negro leaders or organizations that escape the merciless criticism and condemnation of the Negro press are those who stoop to "feed" their graft or who as fellows of the same fold, "scratch each other's backs." To be honest and upright is to bring down upon your head the heavy hammer of condemnation, as such an attitude would "spoil" the game of the "gang" to enrich itself off the ignorance of the masses who are generally led by these newspapers, their editors and friends.

When I arrived in this country in 1916, I discovered that the Negro press had no constructive policy. The news published were all of the kind that reflected the worst of the race's character in murder, adultery, robbery, etc. These crimes were announced in the papers on front pages by glaring and catchy headlines; other features played up by the papers were dancing and parlor socials of questionable intent, and long columns of what is generally called "social" or "society" news of "Mrs. Mary Jones entertained at lunch last evening Mr. So and So" and "Mr. and Mrs. John Brown had the pleasure of entertaining last evening at their elaborate apartment Miss Minnie Baker after which she met a party of friends." Miss Minnie Baker probably was some Octoroon of questionable morals, but made a fuss of because of her "color," and thus runs the kind of material that made up the average Negro newspaper until the Negro World arrived on the scene.

"The Chicago Defender," that has become my arch enemy in the newspaper field, is so, because in 1918–1919 I started the "Negro World" to preserve the term Negro to the race as against the desperate desire of other newspapermen to substitute the term "colored" for the race. Nearly all the newspapers of the race had entered into a conspiracy to taboo the term "Negro" and popularize the term "colored" as the proper race term. To augment this they also fostered the propaganda of bleaching out black skins to light complexions, and straightening out kinky or curly hair to meet the "standard" of the new "society" that was being promoted. I severely criticised "The Chicago Defender" for publishing humiliating and vicious advertisements against the pride and integrity of the race. At that time the "Defender" was publishing full page advertisements about "bleaching the skin" and "straightening the hair." One of these advertisements was from the Plough Manufacturing Company of Tennessee made up as follows:

There were many degrading exhortations to the race to change its black complexion as an entrant to society. There were pictures of two women, one black and the other very bright and under the picture of the black woman appeared these words: "Lighten your black skin," indicating perfection to be reached by bleaching white like the light woman. There were other advertisements such as "Bleach your dark skin," "take the black out of your face," "If you want to be in society lighten your black skin," "Have a light complexion and be in society," "Light skin beauty over night," "Amazing bleach works under skin," "The only harmless way to bleach the skin white," "The most wonderful skin whitener," "Straighten your kinky hair," "Take the kink out of your hair and be in society," "Knock the kink out," "Straighten hair in five days," etc. These advertisements could also be found in any of the Negro papers published all over the country influencing the poor, unthinking masses to be dissatisfied with their race and color, and to "aspire" to look white so as to be in society. I attacked this vicious propaganda and brought down upon my head the damnation of the "leaders" who sought to make a new race and a monkey out of the Negro.

"The Negro World" has rendered a wonderful service to Negro journalism in the United States. It has gradually changed the tone and make-up of some of the papers, and where in 1914–15–16 there was no tendency to notice matters of great importance, today several of the papers are publishing international news and writing intelligent editorials on pertinent subjects. It has been a long and costly fight to bring this about.

I do hope that the statements of truth I have made will further help to bring about a reorganization of the Negro press. I fully realize that very little can be achieved by way of improvement for the race when its press is controlled by crafty and unscrupulous persons who have no pride or love of race.

We need crusaders in journalism who will not seek to enrich themselves off the crimes and ignorance of our race, but men and women who will risk everything for the promotion of racial pride, self respect, love and integrity. The mistake the race is making is to accept and believe that our unprincipled newspaper editors and publishers are our leaders, some of them are our biggest crooks and defamers.

Situated as we are, in a civilization of prejudice and contempt, it is not for us to inspire and advertise the vices of our people, but, by proper leadership, to form characters that would reflect the highest credit upon us and win the highest opinion of an observant and critical world.

6

Redeeming the African Motherland[1]

A major element in Garvey's thought was the necessity for Negroes everywhere to unite in the creation of a strong Negro state in Africa that would eventually assure the redemption of the African motherland. Garvey continued to stress this black Zionism throughout his life, and indeed even increased his emphasis on Africa after his various self-help schemes, such as the Black Star Line, ran into financial difficulty. He shrewdly recognized that Africa was not only a valuable symbol of a proud Negro heritage but was also the means to unify the scattered black diaspora for the future achievements of the Negro race. The following speech, delivered in Liberty Hall in Harlem during the second international U.N.I.A. convention in August, 1921, is representative of Garvey's lifelong belief in the importance of Africa for black men and women everywhere.

Four years ago, realizing the oppression and the hardships from which we suffered, we organized ourselves into an organization for the purpose of bettering our condition, and founding a government of our own. The four years of organization have brought good results, in that from an obscure, despised race we have grown into a mighty power, a mighty force whose influence is being felt throughout the length and breadth of the world. The Universal Negro Improvement Association existed but in name four years ago, today it is known as the greatest moving force among Negroes. We have accomplished this through unity of effort and unity of purpose, it is a fair demonstration of what we will be able to accomplish in the very near future, when the millions who are outside the pale of the Universal Negro Improvement Association will have linked themselves up with us.

By our success of the last four years we will be able to estimate the

[1] From Amy Jacques Garvey, ed., *Philosophy and Opinioins of Marcus Garvey*, vol. I (New York: Universal Publishing House, 1923), pp. 71–74. Reprinted by permission of Amy Jacques Garvey.

grander success of a free and redeemed Africa. In climbing the heights
to where we are today, we have had to surmount difficulties, we have
had to climb over obstacles, but the obstacles were stepping stones to
the future greatness of this Cause we represent. Day by day we are
writing a new history, recording new deeds of valor performed by this
race of ours. It is true that the world has not yet valued us at our true
worth but we are climbing up so fast and with such force that every
day the world is changing its attitude towards us. Wheresoever you
turn your eyes today you will find the moving influence of the Universal Negro Improvement Association among Negroes from all corners of
the globe. We hear among Negroes the cry of "Africa for the Africans".
This cry has become a positive, determined one. It is a cry that is raised
simultaneously the world over because of the universal oppression that
affects the Negro. You who are congregated here tonight as Delegates
representing the hundreds of branches of the Universal Negro Improvement Association in different parts of the world will realize that we in
New York are positive in this great desire of a free and redeemed
Africa. We have established this Liberty Hall as the centre from which
we send out the sparks of liberty to the four corners of the globe, and
if you have caught the spark in your section, we want you to keep it
a-burning for the great Cause we represent.

There is a mad rush among races everywhere towards national independence. Everywhere we hear the cry of liberty, of freedom, and a
demand for democracy. In our corner of the world we are raising the
cry for liberty, freedom and democracy. Men who have raised the cry
for freedom and liberty in ages past have always made up their minds
to die for the realization of the dream. We who are assembled in this
Convention as Delegates representing the Negroes of the world give out
the same spirit that the fathers of liberty in this country gave out over
one hundred years ago. We give out a spirit that knows no compromise,
a spirit that refuses to turn back, a spirit that says "Liberty or Death",
and in prosecution of this great ideal—the ideal of a free and redeemed
Africa—men may scorn, men may spurn us, and may say that we are
on the wrong side of life, but let me tell you that way in which you
are travelling is just the way all peoples who are free have travelled in
the past. If you want Liberty you yourselves must strike the blow. If
you must be free you must become so through your own effort, through
your own initiative. Those who have discouraged you in the past are
those who have enslaved you for centuries and it is not expected that
they will admit that you have a right to strike out at this late hour for
freedom, liberty and democracy.

At no time in the history of the world, for the last five hundred years,
was there ever a serious attempt made to free Negroes. We have been
camouflaged into believing that we were made free by Abraham Lin-

coln. That we were made free by Victoria of England, but up to now we are still slaves, we are industrial slaves, we are social slaves, we are political slaves, and the new Negro desires a freedom that has no boundary, no limit. We desire a freedom that will lift us to the common standard of all men, whether they be white men of Europe or yellow men of Asia, therefore, in our desire to lift ourselves to that standard we shall stop at nothing until there is a free and redeemed Africa.

I understand that just at this time while we are endeavoring to create public opinion and public sentiment in favor of a free Africa, that others of our race are being subsidized to turn the attention of the world toward a different desire on the part of Negroes, but let me tell you that we who make up this Organization know no turning back, we have pledged ourselves even unto the last drop of our sacred blood that Africa must be free. The enemy may argue with you to show you the impossibility of a free and redeemed Africa, but I want you to take as your argument the thirteen colonies of America, that once owed their sovereignty to Great Britain, that sovereignty has been destroyed to make a United States of America. George Washington was not God Almighty. He was a man like any Negro in this building, and if he and his associates were able to make a free America, we too can make a free Africa. Hampden, Gladstone, Pitt and Disraeli were not the representatives of God in the person of Jesus Christ. They were but men, but in their time they worked for the expansion of the British Empire, and today they boast of a British Empire upon which "the sun never sets." As Pitt and Gladstone were able to work for the expansion of the British Empire, so you and I can work for the expansion of a great African Empire. Voltaire and Mirabeau were not Jesus Christs, they were but men like ourselves. They worked and overturned the French Monarchy. They worked for the Democracy which France now enjoys, and if they were able to do that, we are able to work for a democracy in Africa. Lenin and Trotsky were not Jesus Christs, but they were able to overthrow the despotism of Russia, and today they have given to the world a Social Republic, the first of its kind. If Lenin and Trotsky were able to do that for Russia, you and I can do that for Africa. Therefore, let no man, let no power on earth, turn you from this sacred cause of liberty. I prefer to die at this moment rather than not to work for the freedom of Africa. If liberty is good for certain sets of humanity it is good for all. Black men, Colored men, Negroes have as much right to be free as any other race that God Almighty ever created, and we desire freedom that is unfettered, freedom that is unlimited, freedom that will give us a chance and opportunity to rise to the fullest of our ambition and that we cannot get in countries where other men rule and dominate.

We have reached the time when every minute, every second must count for something done, something achieved in the cause of Africa. We need the freedom of Africa now, therefore, we desire the kind of leadership that will give it to us as quickly as possible. You will realize that not only individuals, but governments are using their influence against us. But what do we care about the unrighteous influence of any government? Our cause is based upon righteousness. And anything that is not righteous we have no respect for, because God Almighty is our leader and Jesus Christ our standard bearer. We rely on them for that kind of leadership that will make us free, for it is the same God who inspired the Psalmist to write "Princes shall come out of Egypt and Ethiopia shall stretch out her hands unto God". At this moment methinks I see Ethiopia stretching forth her hands unto God and methinks I see the Angel of God taking up the standard of the Red, the Black and the Green, and saying "Men of the Negro Race, Men of Ethiopia, follow me". Tonight we are following. We are following 400,000,000 strong. We are following with a determination that we must be free before the wreck of matter, before the crash of worlds.

It falls to our lot to tear off the shackles that bind Mother Africa. Can you do it? You did it in the Revolutionary War. You did it in the Civil War; You did it at the Battles of the Marne and Verdun; You did it in Mesopotamia. You can do it marching up the battle heights of Africa. Let the world know that 400,000,000 Negroes are prepared to die or live as free men. Despise us as much as you care. Ignore us as much as you care. We are coming 400,000,000 strong. We are coming with our woes behind us, with the memory of suffering behind us— woes and suffering of three hundred years—they shall be our inspiration. My bulwark of strength in the conflict for freedom in Africa, will be the three hundred years of persecution and hardship left behind in this Western Hemisphere. The more I remember the suffering of my fore-fathers, the more I remember the lynchings and burnings in the Southern States of America, the more I will fight on even though the battle seems doubtful. Tell me that I must turn back, and I laugh you to scorn. Go on! Go on! Climb ye the heights of liberty and cease not in well doing until you have planted the banner of the Red, the Black and the Green on the hilltops of Africa.

7

Garvey's Message for Whites[1]

Believing the United States to be a nation that would always be dominated by whites, Garvey put little stock in the efforts by such organizations as the National Association for the Advancement of Colored People to secure equal rights for American Negroes. White Americans would never freely grant equal opportunities and treatment to blacks, he argued, nor should sensible blacks expect them to. The solution was a Negro state in Africa, in which black men and women could develop their own institutions and civilization. Such doctrine was of course bitter heresy to those black leaders, notably W. E. B. DuBois of the NAACP, who were striving for Negro civil rights in an integrated society, and they quickly launched a campaign to discredit Garvey. He in turn tried to counter this opposition from black intellectuals and publicists by persuading white Americans of the importance of his movement in resolving the longstanding race issue in America.

AIMS AND OBJECTS OF MOVEMENT FOR SOLUTION OF NEGRO PROBLEM

Generally the public is kept misinformed of the truth surrounding new movements of reform. Very seldom, if ever, reformers get the truth told about them and their movements. Because of this natural attitude, the Universal Negro Improvement Association has been greatly handicapped in its work, causing thereby one of the most liberal and helpful human movements of the twentieth century to be held up to ridicule by those who take pride in poking fun at anything not already successfully established.

The white man of America has become the natural leader of the world. He, because of his exalted position, is called upon to help in all human efforts. From nations to individuals the appeal is made to

[1] From Amy Jacques Garvey, ed., *Philosophy and Opinions of Marcus Garvey*, vol. II (New York: Universal Publishing House, 1926), pp. 37–41, 42–43. Reprinted by permission of Amy Jacques Garvey.

him for aid in all things affecting humanity, so, naturally, there can be no great mass movement or change without first acquainting the leader on whose sympathy and advice the world moves.

It is because of this, and more so because of a desire to be Christian friends with the white race, why I explain the aims and objects of the Universal Negro Improvement Association.

The Universal Negro Improvement Association is an organization among Negroes that is seeking to improve the condition of the race, with the view of establishing a nation in Africa where Negroes will be given the opportunity to develop by themselves, without creating the hatred and animosity that now exist in countries of the white race through Negroes rivaling them for the highest and best positions in government, politics, society and industry. The organization believes in the rights of all men, yellow, white and black. To us, the white race has a right to the peaceful possession and occupation of countries of its own and in like manner the yellow and black races have their rights. It is only by an honest and liberal consideration of such rights can the world be blessed with the peace that is sought by Christian teachers and leaders.

THE SPIRITUAL BROTHERHOOD OF MAN

The following preamble to the constitution of the organization speaks for itself:

"The Universal Negro Improvement Association and African Communities' League is a social, friendly, humanitarian, charitable, educational, institutional, constructive, and expansive society, and is founded by persons, desiring to the utmost to work for the general uplift of the Negro peoples of the world. And the members pledge themselves to do all in their power to conserve the rights of their noble race and to respect the rights of all mankind, believing always in the Brotherhood of Man and the Fatherhood of God. The motto of the organization is: One God! One Aim! One Destiny! Therefore, let justice be done to all mankind, realizing that if the strong oppresses the weak confusion and discontent will ever mark the path of man, but with love, faith and charity toward all the reign of peace and plenty will be heralded into the world and the generations of men shall be called Blessed."

The declared objects of the association are:

"To establish a Universal Confraternity among the race; to promote the spirit of pride and love; to reclaim the fallen; to administer to and assist the needy; to assist in civilizing the backward tribes of Africa; to assist in the development of Independent Negro Nations and Communities; to establish a central nation for the race; to establish Commissaries or Agencies in the principal countries and cities of the world for the representation of all Negroes; to promote a conscientious Spiritual worship among the native tribes of Africa; to establish Universities, Colleges, Academies and Schools for the racial education and culture of the people; to work for better conditions among Negroes everywhere."

SUPPLYING A LONG-FELT WANT

The organization of the Universal Negro Improvement Association has supplied among Negroes a long-felt want. Hitherto the other Negro movements in America, with the exception of the Tuskegee effort of Booker T. Washington, sought to teach the Negro to aspire to social equality with the white, meaning thereby the right to intermarry and fraternize in every social way. This has been the source of much trouble and still some Negro organizations continue to preach this dangerous "race destroying doctrine' added to a program of political agitation and aggression. The Universal Negro Improvement Association on the other hand believes in and teaches the pride and purity of race. We believe that the white race should uphold its racial pride and perpetuate itself, and that the black race should do likewise. We believe that there is room enough in the world for the various race groups to grow and develop by themselves without seeking to destroy the Creator's plan by the constant introduction of mongrel types.

The unfortunate condition of slavery, as imposed upon the Negro, and which caused the mongrelization of the race, should not be legalized and continued now to the harm and detriment of both races.

The time has really come to give the Negro a chance to develop himself to a moral-standard-man, and it is for such an opportunity that the Universal Negro Improvement Association seeks in the creation of an African nation for Negroes, where the greatest latitude would be given to work out this racial ideal.

There are hundreds of thousands of colored people in America who desire race amalgamation and miscegenation as a solution of the race problem. These people are, therefore, opposed to the race pride ideas of black and white; but the thoughtful of both races will naturally ignore the ravings of such persons and honestly work for the solution of a problem that has been forced upon us.

Liberal white America and race loving Negroes are bound to think at this time and thus evolve a program or plan by which there can be a fair and amicable settlement of the question.

We cannot put off the consideration of the matter, for time is pressing on our hands. The educated Negro is making rightful constitutional demands. The great white majority will never grant them, and thus we march on to danger if we do not now stop and adjust the matter.

The time is opportune to regulate the relationship between both races. Let the Negro have a country of his own. Help him to return to his original home, Africa, and there give him the opportunity to climb from the lowest to the highest positions in a state of his own. If not, then the nation will have to hearken to the demand of the aggressive, "social equality" organization, known as the National Association for the Advancement of Colored People, of which W. E. B. DuBois is leader, which declares vehemently for social and political equality, viz.: Negroes and whites in the same hotels, homes, residential districts, public and private places, a Negro as president, members of the Cabinet, Governors of States, Mayors of cities, and leaders of society in the United States. In this agitation, DuBois is ably supported by the "Chicago Defender," a colored newspaper published in Chicago. This paper advocates Negroes in the Cabinet and Senate. All these, as everybody knows, are the Negroes' constitutional rights, but reason dictates that the masses of the white race will never stand by the ascendency of an opposite minority group to the favored positions in a government, society and industry that exist by the will of the majority, hence the demand of the DuBois group of colored leaders will only lead, ultimately, to further disturbances in riots, lynching and mob rule. The only logical solution therefore, is to supply the Negro with opportunities and environments of his own, and there point him to the fullness of his ambition.

NEGROES WHO SEEK SOCIAL EQUALITY

The Negro who seeks the White House in America could find ample play for his ambition in Africa. The Negro who seeks the office of Secretary of State in America would have a fair chance of demonstrating his diplomacy in Africa. The Negro who seeks a seat in the Senate or of being governor of a State in America, would be provided with a glorious chance for statesmanship in Africa.

The Negro has a claim on American white sympathy that cannot be denied. The Negro has labored for 300 years in contributing to America's greatness. White America will not be unmindful, therefore, of this consideration, but will treat him kindly. Yet it is realized that all human beings have a limit to their humanity. The humanity of white America, we realize, will seek self-protection and self-preservation, and that is why the thoughtful and reasonable Negro sees no hope in America for satisfying the aggressive program of the National Association for the Advancement of Colored People, but advances the reasonable plan of the Universal Negro Improvement Association, that of creating in Africa a nation and government for the Negro race.

This plan when properly undertaken and prosecuted will solve the race problem in America in fifty years. Africa affords a wonderful opportunity at the present time for colonization by the Negroes of the Western world. There is Liberia, already established as an independent Negro government. Let white America assist Afro-Americans to go there and help develop the country. Then, there are the late German colonies; let white sentiment force England and France to turn them over to the American and West Indian Negroes who fought for the Allies in the World's War. Then, France, England and Belgium owe America billions of dollars which they claim they cannot afford to repay immediately. Let them compromise by turning over Sierra Leone and the Ivory Coast on the West Coast of Africa and add them to Liberia and help make Liberia a state worthy of her history.

The Negroes of Africa and America are one in blood. They have sprung from the same common stock. They can work and live together and thus make their own racial contribution to the world.

Will deep thinking and liberal white America help? It is a considerate duty.

It is true that a large number of self-seeking colored agitators and so-called political leaders, who hanker after social equality and fight for the impossible in politics and governments, will rave, but remember that the slave-holder raved, but the North said, "Let the slaves go free"; the British Parliament raved when the Colonists said, "We want a free and American nation"; the Monarchists of France raved when the people declared for a more liberal form of government.

The masses of Negroes think differently from the self-appointed leaders of the race. The majority of Negro leaders are selfish, self-appointed and not elected by the people. The people desire freedom in a land of their own, while the colored politician desires office and social equality for himself in America, and that is why we are asking white America to help the masses to realize their objective. . . .

Surely the time has come for the Negro to look homeward. He has won civilization and Christianity at the price of slavery. The Negro who is thoughtful and serviceable, feels that God intended him to give to his brothers still in darkness, the light of his civilization. The very light element of Negroes do not want to go back to Africa. They believe that in time, through miscegenation, the American race will be of their type. This is a fallacy and in that respect the agitation of the mulatto leader, Dr. W. E. B. DuBois and the National Association for the Advancement of Colored People is dangerous to both races.

The off-colored people, being children of the Negro race, should combine to re-establish the purity of their own race, rather than seek to perpetuate the abuse of both races. That is to say, all elements of the Negro race should be encouraged to get together and form themselves into a healthy whole, rather than seeking to lose their identities through miscegenation and social intercourse with the white race. These statements are made because we desire an honest solution of the problem and no flattery or deception will bring that about.

Let the white and Negro people settle down in all seriousness and in true sympathy and solve the problem. When that is done, a new day of peace and good will will be ushered in.

The natural opponents among Negroes to a program of this kind are that lazy element who believe always in following the line of least resistance, being of themselves void of initiative and the pioneering spirit to do for themselves. The professional Negro leader and the class who are agitating for social equality feel that it is too much work for them to settle down and build up a civilization of their own. They feel it is easier to seize on to the civilization of the white man and under the guise of constitutional rights fight for those things that the white man has created. Natural reason suggests that the white man will not yield them, hence such leaders are but fools for their pains. Teach the Negro to do for himself, help him the best way possible in that direction; but to encourage him into the belief that he is going to possess himself of the things that others have fought and died for, is to build up in his mind false hopes never to be realized. As for instance, Dr. W. E. B. DuBois, who has been educated by white charity, is a brilliant scholar, but he is not a hard worker. He prefers to use his higher intellectual abilities to fight for a place among white men in society, industry and in politics, rather than use that ability to work and create for his own race that which the race could be able to take credit for. He would not think of repeating for his race the work of the Pilgrim Fathers or the Colonists who laid the foundation of America, but he prefers to fight and agitate for the privilege of dancing with a white lady at a ball at the Biltmore or at the Astoria hotels in New York. That kind of leadership will destroy the Negro in America and against which the Universal Negro Improvement Association is fighting.

The Universal Negro Improvement Association is composed of all shades of Negroes—blacks, mulattoes and yellows—who are all working honestly for the purification of their race, and for a sympathetic adjustment of the race problem.

8
Advice to Black Workers[1]

Garvey's racial views made him skeptical of any pro-
posals to achieve Negro betterment along interracial class lines.
He suspected that white Socialists and Communists were at heart
just as prejudiced against black people as were other whites, and
he doubted that white trade unionists would willingly share their
job opportunities and union benefits with black workers. For the
moment, he thought, the best friend of Negro workers was the
white capitalist, whose self-interest would lead him to use black
labor if it was cheap enough. Until Negroes could acquire enough
capital and solidarity to create their own jobs, therefore, they
must beware of white-led worker movements, which would in all
likelihood undermine the marginal foothold of blacks in Ameri-
can industry. Garvey much preferred the outspoken white racism
of the Ku Klux Klan and similar groups to what he assumed was
the hypocrisy of those white reformers who were undermining
black unity by holding out hope for the impossible dream of
equality.

**THE NEGRO, COMMUNISM, TRADE UNIONISM, AND HIS (?) FRIEND:
"BEWARE OF GREEKS BEARING GIFTS"**

If I must advise the Negro workingman and laborer, I should
warn him against the present brand of Communism or Workers' Parti-
zanship as taught in America, and to be careful of the traps and pitfalls
of white trade unionism, in affiliation with the American Federation
of white workers or laborers.

It seems strange and a paradox, but the only convenient friend the
Negro worker or laborer has, in America, at the present time, is the
white capitalist. The capitalist being selfish—seeking only the largest
profit out of labor—is willing and glad to use Negro labor wherever
possible on a scale "reasonably" below the standard white union wage.

[1] From Amy Jacques Garvey, ed., *Philosophy and Opinions of Marcus Garvey*,
vol. II (New York: Universal Publishing House, 1926), pp. 69–71. Reprinted by permission of Amy Jacques Garvey.

He will tolerate the Negro in any industry (except those that are necessarily guarded for the protection of the whiteman's material, racial and assumed cultural dominance) if he accepts a lower standard of wage than the white union man; but, if the Negro unionizes himself to the level of the white worker, and, in affiliation with him, the choice and preference of employment is given to the white worker, without any regard or consideration for the Negro.

White Unionism is now trying to rope in the Negro and make him a standard wage worker, then, when it becomes generally known that he demands the same wage as the white worker, an appeal or approach will be made to the white capitalist or employer, to alienate his sympathy or consideration for the Negro, causing him, in the face of all things being equal, to discriminate in favor of the white worker as a race duty and obligation. In this respect the Negro if not careful to play his game well, which must be done through and by his leaders, is between "hell and the powder house."

The danger of Communism to the Negro, in countries where he forms the minority of the population, is seen in the selfish and vicious attempts of that party or group to use the Negro's vote and physical numbers in helping to smash and over-throw, by revolution, a system that is injurious to them as the white under dogs, the success of which would put their majority group or race still in power, not only as communists but as whitemen. To me there is no difference between two roses looking alike, and smelling alike, even if some one calls them by different names. Fundamentally what racial difference is there between a white Communist, Republican or Democrat? On the appeal of race interest the Communist is as ready as either to show his racial ascendancy or superiority over the Negro. He will be as quick and eager as any to show the Negro that he is white, and by Divine right of assumption has certain duties to perform to the rest of us mortals, and to defend and protect certain racial ideals against the barbarian hordes that threaten white supremacy.

I am of the opinion that the group of whites from whom Communists are made, in America, as well as trade unionists and members of the Worker's party, is more dangerous to the Negro's welfare than any other group at present. Lynching mobs and wild time parties are generally made up of 99½ per cent. of such white people. The Negro should keep shy of Communism or the Worker's party in America. Since they are so benevolent let them bring about their own reforms and show us how different they are to others. We have been bitten too many times by all the other parties,—"Once bitten, twice shy"—Negroes have no right with white people's fights or quarrels, except, like the humble, hungry, meagre dog, to run off with the bone when both contestants drop it, being sure to separate himself from the big, well fed dogs, by a good distance, otherwise to be overtaken, and then completely outdone.

If the Negro takes my advice he will organize by himself and always keep his scale of wage a little lower than the whites until he is able to become, through proper leadership, his own employer; by so doing he will keep the good will of the white employer and live a little longer under the present scheme of things. If not, between Communism, white trade unionism and worker's parties he is doomed in the next 25, 50 or 100 years to complete economic and general extermination.

The Negro needs to be saved from his (?) "Friends," and beware of "Greeks bearing gifts." The greatest enemies of the Negro are among those who hypocritically profess love and fellowship for him, when, in truth, and deep down in their hearts, they despise and hate him. Pseudo-philanthropists and their organizations are killing the Negro. White men and women of the Morefield Storey, Joel Spingarn, Julius Rosenwald, Oswald Garrison Villard, Congressman Dyer and Mary White Ovington type, in conjunction with the above mentioned agencies, are disarming, dis-visioning, dis-ambitioning and fooling the Negro to death. They teach the Negro to look to the whites in a false direction. They, by their practices are endeavoring to hold the Negroes in check, as a possible dangerous minority group, and yet point them to the impossible dream of equality that shall never materialize, as they well know, and never intended; at the same time distracting the Negro from the real solution and objective of securing nationalism. By thus decoying and deceiving the Negro and side-tracking his real objective, they hope to gain time against him in allowing others of their race to perfect the plan by which the blacks are to be completely destroyed as a competitive permanent part of white majority civilization and culture. They have succeeded in enslaving the ignorance of a small group of so-called "Negro intellectuals" whom they use as agents to rope in the unsuspicious colored or Negro people. They have become resentful and bitter toward the Ku Klux Klan, and use the influence of their controlled newspapers (white and colored) to fight them, not because they so much hate the Klan, where the Negro is concerned, but because the Klan, through an honest expression of the whiteman's attitude toward the Negro, prepares him to help himself.

This hypocritical group of whites, like Spingarn and Storey, have succeeded an earlier group that fooled the Negro during the days of Reconstruction. Instead of pointing the Negro to Africa, as Jefferson and Lincoln did, they sought to revenge him, for the new liberty given him, by imprisoning him in the whiteman's civilization; to further rob his labor, and exploit his ignorance, until he is subsequently ground to death by a newly developed superior white civilization. The plot of these Negro baiters is wretched to contemplate, hence their hatred of me and their influence to crush me in my attempt to save the black race.

Between the Ku Klux Klan and the Morefield Storey National Association for the Advancement of "Colored" People group, give me the Klan for their honesty of purpose towards the Negro. They are better friends to my race, for telling us what they are, and what they mean, thereby giving us a chance to stir for ourselves, than all the hypocrites put together with their false gods and religions, notwithstanding. Religions that they preach and will not practise; a God they talk about, whom they abuse every day—away with the farce, hypocrisy and lie. It smells, it stinks to high heaven. I regard the Klan, the Anglo-Saxon Clubs and White America Societies, as far as the Negro is concerned, as better friends of the race than all other groups of hypocritical whites put together. I like honesty and fair play. You may call me a Klansman if you will, but, potentially, every whiteman is a Klansman, as far as the Negro in competition with whites socially, economically and politically is concerned, and there is no use lying about it.

9

The Collapse of Garvey's Dream[1]

Garvey's blunt criticism of many of the existing Negro groups and leaders, and their resentment of his ability to reach and organize the black masses to an unprecedented degree, led to a concerted drive by his enemies to discredit this brash upstart Jamaican. Garvey was vulnerable to charges of financial misman-agement because most of his grandiose business ventures, espe-cially the Black Star Line, were foundering despite his remarkable success in raising large funds from his loyal followers. Responding to editorial agitation in the Negro press and to complaints from some disgruntled Black Star stockholders, in January 1922 federal officials arrested Garvey on a charge of using the mails to defraud. Brought to trial and convicted the following year, he served nearly three years of a five-year sentence in Atlanta Penitentiary before President Coolidge commuted his remaining time and or-dered him deported to Jamaica late in 1927. The following two selections show Garvey's indomitable spirit in this period of ad-versity: the first is his closing address to the jury at his trial, and the second, his initial message to his followers after he began serving his prison sentence in February 1925.

CLOSING ADDRESS TO THE JURY

Gentlemen, we come to the point where this Black Star Line was said to be bankrupt. Bankruptcy papers were never filed against the Black Star Line. The Black Star Line had times when it might not have been in the best financial condition, but no one had filed any papers for bankruptcy. We had liabilities and assets not only in money, not only in property, but the good will of the people, which was the greatest asset, and if somebody had not taken the funds and dissatisfied the people about that boat, we would have been a success.

Where did the Black Star Line get money to buy the Yarmouth?

[1] From Amy Jacques Garvey, ed., *Philosophy and Opinions of Marcus Garvey*, vol. II (New York: Universal Publishing House, 1926), pp. 211–16, 237–39. Reprinted by permission of Amy Jacques Garvey.

From the same people who would have been willing to buy the other boats. When we bought the Yarmouth we had no assets other than the good will of the people, and they subscribed the money to buy the Yarmouth, and the Kanawha and the Shady Side. If the people did that, then would not they have done more? They would have given one-half more if they had to acquire that African ship, but they were told the ship would be here tomorrow. Tomorrow never came, and the people, who were the assets, became doubtful and we could have no ships.

When Garvey was in the West Indies over $30,000 was wasted. If the management had signed a proper contract with Morse we probably would have had the ship Kanawha in different condition. It was not so much the money, but intelligence and brain. We started the organization with only 13 members, and today we have an organization of six million members throughout the world with 900 branches.

We had no monetary considerations or reward before us, but the good we could do for our race, for this and succeeding generations. Those of us who started the work did not think about salary of $50 a week. We thought of giving what we could in body and soul for the emancipation of a race and for our country. I hardly believe you understand the situation. You will say it was bad business. But, gentlemen, there is something spiritual beside business. You will say that we sold $800,000, in stock. They ought to have good ships. Did we get all that money at the same time? And during the time we were gathering this money we had to invest and carry on and show good faith. We had to pay in parts on the Kanawha and Shady Side. If we had all the money at the one time we could have bought one of the best ships in this country.

When we made our purchase the tonnage on ships was high. When we were supposed to have bought the Phyllis Wheatley tonnage had fallen, ships were going practically for nothing. If we were able to get ships during the war, we would have gotten ships then, when shipping had fallen in this country, as low as the price went. The Shipping Board had numbers of ships. The failure of the Black Star Line was only a drop in the bucket. You had numbers of failures among your own race, gentlemen. Your experts failed by the hundreds and during the period the Black Star Line had the difficulties the Shipping Board of the United States lost $300,000,000. Was there fraud on the part of the Shipping Board in the use of the millions? The taxes, your money and my money, were converted into ships and the ships failed. Did we indict our great President for the use of the millions? Sometimes to fail is but stepping stones to greater things.

The Universal Negro Improvement Association and the Black Star Line employs thousands of black girls and black boys. Girls who could only be washer women in your homes, we made clerks and stenographers of them in the Black Star Line's office. You will see that from the start we tried to dignify our race. If I am to be condemned for that I am satisfied.

I Am a Negro

I am a Negro. I make absolutely no apology for being a Negro because my God created me to be what I am, and as I am so will I return to my God, for He knows just why He created me as He did. So, gentlemen, you will understand that behind the whole business proposition lies the spirit of the movement. I have no time to go into the work of the Universal Negro Improvement Association, but I say this: I know there are certain people who do not like me because I am black; they don't like me because I am not born here, though no fault of mine.

I didn't bring myself into this western world. You know the history of my race. I was brought here; I was sold to some slave master in the island of Jamaica. Some Irish slave master who subsequently gave my great-grandfather his name. Garvey is not an African name; it is an Irish name, as Johnston is not an African name, Garcia is not an African name, Thompson and Tobias are not African names. Where did we get those names from? We inherited them from our own slave masters, English, French, Irish or Scotch. So, if I was born in Jamaica, it was no fault of mine. It was because that slave ship which took me to Jamaica did not come to American ports. That is how some Negroes of America were not born in the West Indies.

We did not come here of our own free will. We were brought here, and so the question of birth does not enter into the question of the Negro. It was a matter of accident. Will you blame me for the accident of being a Jamaican Negro and not an American Negro? Surely you will not. But there is a bigger question involved. It is a question of race. What are you going to do with this question of race? You may sit quietly by, but it is going to be serious later on, and that is why the Universal Negro Improvement Association is endeavoring to assist you in solving the Negro problem by helping the Negro to become enterprising, independent politically, and by having a country of his own. If you follow me down the ages you will see within a hundred years you are going to have a terrible race problem in America, when you will have increased and the country will become over-populated. It will be a fight for existence between two opposite races. The weak will have to go down in defeat before the strong. In the riots of Washington, East St. Louis, Chicago, Tulsa, study the race question and you will find that some serious thinking must be done now to solve this problem; otherwise our children will be confronted with it.

Do you know when you want bread and the other fellow wants it, when there is only one loaf—what is going to happen? Enmity and pressure is going to spring up and a fight will ensue. That is why the Universal Negro Improvement Association has started this proposition to redeem Africa and build up a country of our own, so as not to molest you in the country your fathers founded hundreds of years ago.

Some Negroes believe in social equality. They want to intermarry with the white women of this country, and it is going to cause trouble later on. Some Negroes want the same jobs you have. They want to be presidents of the nation. What is going to be the outcome? Study the race question and you will find that the program of the Universal Negro Improvement Association and the Black Star Line is the solution of the problem which confronts us, not only in this country, but throughout the world.

Folks try to misrepresent me and say I don't like white people. That is not true. Some of the best friends I have are white men. The bishop who testified here has been my friend from youth. He said other things that some of us did not understand. I asked him, Do you know Marcus Garvey?—he said yes. What is the opinion of him? He said doubtful. Now probably you didn't understand what he meant. Garvey was a public man. Opinions differ. He was a priest and he had to tell the truth. Surely some men are doubtful of Marcus Garvey, and there are some who are not doubtful. He didn't say that Garvey was doubtful. He gives it as it was, when I asked him about his personal opinion I was not allowed because it was not the proper question, the court ruled. He said, however, Garvey was a worthy man, so I trust you will not have the wrong impression.

A Heart Untainted

Now, gentlemen, I will not touch on the other witnesses, I leave it all to you. But, gentlemen, remember this, I assure you that you are all at this time to judge a man, to judge me by the testimony, by what has been brought here, by your judgment of what is right and what is wrong. You condemn the body but not the soul. It is not in your power to condemn a soul, it is only the power of God. You can only condemn the body, but God condemns the soul. Yes, judge me and God will judge you for judging Marcus Garvey. You can believe me, it is satisfactory to Marcus Garvey because some writer says, "What greater breastplate than a heart untainted. Thrice is he armed who hath his quarrel just and he but naked—though locked up in steel whose conscience with injustice is corrupted." I stand before you and the honorable court for your judgment and I do not regret what I have done for the Universal Negro Improvement Association; for the Negro race, because I did it from the fullness of my soul. I did it with the fear of my God, believing that I was doing the right thing. I am still firm in my belief that I served my race, people, conscience and God. I further make no apology for what I have done. I ask for no mercy. If you say I am guilty, I go to my God as I feel, a clear conscience and a clean soul, knowing I have not wronged even a child of my race or any member of my family. I love all mankind. I love Jew, Gentile, I love white and black.

I have respect for every race. I believe the Irish should be free; they should have a country. I believe the Jew should be free and the Egyptian should be free, and the Indian and the Poles. I believe also that the black man should be free. I would fight for the freedom of the Jew, the Irish, the Poles; I would fight and die for the liberation of 400,000,000 Negroes. I expect from the world for Negroes what the world expects from them.

I thank you for your patience, gentlemen, and his Honor for the patience he has exhibited also. There has been some differences, but I have great respect for this court. I respect the constitution of this great country, the most liberal constitution in the world. This great government, the most liberal in the world. Could I go to Washington without paying my homage and respect to that hero, George Washington, and Abraham Lincoln, the emancipator of our million slaves? Then, how dare anyone accuse me of being disrespectful to the United States or the courts—I feel that my rights are infringed upon. If I differed from the judge, it is but human. I know you are business men just as I am. My business has been going to pieces and I know how much yours is going to pieces, but if you were to be tried and I were a juror I would give you the same consideration as you have given me, therefore, I leave myself to you, feeling that you should judge me as your God shall judge you, not for friendship, not for satisfying the whims of someone, but because of truth and justice.

The District Attorney will tell you it is Garvey, Garvey, Garvey, Garvey is the master mind, Garvey is the genius; Garvey is but a man. Garvey is but human. But Garvey must be destroyed, but in destroying the physical in Garvey, you cannot destroy the soul and I feel you, gentlemen, will not do anything except that which is prompted by justice, truth and the law, as you know the law is but an expression of truth, of justice, and of thought. The law demands truth and justice so that justice can be done.

I leave myself to you. I have not denied anything that I know of and have done.

FIRST MESSAGE TO THE NEGROES OF THE WORLD
FROM ATLANTA PRISON

February 10, 1925.

Fellow Men of the Negro Race, Greeting:

I am delighted to inform you, that your humble servant is as happy in suffering from you and our cause as is possible under the circumstances of being viciously outraged by a group of plotters who have connived to do their worst to humiliate you through me, in the fight for real emancipation and African Redemption.

I do trust that you have given no credence to the vicious lies of white and enemy newspapers and those who have spoken in reference to my surrender. The liars plotted in every way to make it appear that I was not willing to surrender to the court. My attorney advised me that no mandate would have been handed down for ten or fourteen days, as is the custom of the courts, and that would have given me time to keep speaking engagements I had in Detroit, Cincinnati and Cleveland. I hadn't left the city for ten hours when the liars flashed the news that I was a fugitive. That was good news to circulate all over the world to demoralize the millions of Negroes in America, Africa, Asia, the West Indies and Central America, but the idiots ought to know by now that they can't fool all the Negroes at the same time.

I do not want at this time to write anything that would make it difficult for you to meet the opposition of the enemy without my assistance. Suffice it to say that the history of the outrage shall form a splendid chapter in the history of Africa redeemed, when black men will no longer be under the heels of others, but have a civilization and country of their own.

The whole affair is a disgrace, and the whole black world knows it. We shall not forget. Our day may be fifty, a hundred or two hundred years ahead, but let us watch, work and pray, for the civilization of injustice is bound to crumble and bring destruction down upon the heads of the unjust.

The idiots thought that they could humiliate me personally, but in that they are mistaken. The minutes of suffering are counted, and when God and Africa come back and measure out retribution these minutes may multiply by thousands for the sinners. Our Arab and Riffian friends will be ever vigilant, as the rest of Africa and ourselves shall be. Be assured that I planted well the seed of Negro or black nationalism which cannot be destroyed even by the foul play that has been meted out to me.

Continue to pray for me and I shall ever be true to my trust. I want you, the black peoples of the world, to know that W. E. B. DuBois and that vicious Negro-hating organization known as the Association for the Advancement of "Colored" People are the greatest enemies the black people have in the world. I have so much to do in the few minutes at my disposal that I cannot write exhaustively on this or any other matter, but be warned against these two enemies. Don't allow them to fool you with fine sounding press releases, speeches and books; they are the vipers who have planned with others the extinction of the "black" race.

My work is just begun, and when the history of my suffering is complete, then future generations of Negroes will have in their hands the guide by which they shall know the "sins" of the twentieth century. I, and I know you, too, believe in time, and we shall wait patiently for two hundred years, if need be, to face our enemies through our posterity.

You will cheer me much if you will now do even more for the organization than when I was among you. Hold up the hands of those who are carrying on. Help them to make good, so that the work may continue to spread from pole to pole.

I am also making a last minute appeal for support to the Black Cross Navigation and Trading Company. Please send in and make your loans so as to enable the directors to successfully carry on the work.

All I have I have given to you. I have sacrificed my home and my loving wife for you. I entrust her to your charge, to protect and defend her in my absence. She is the bravest little woman I know. She has suffered and sacrificed with me for you; therefore, please do not desert her at this dismal hour, when she stands alone. I have left her penniless and helpless to face the world, because I gave you all, but her courage is great, and I know she will hold up for you and me.

After my enemies are satisfied, in life or death I shall come back to you to serve even as I have served before. In life I shall be the same; in death I shall be a terror to the foes of Negro liberty. If death has power, then count on me in death to be the real Marcus Garvey I would like to be. If I may come in an earthquake, or a cyclone, or plague, or pestilence, or as God would have me, then be assured that I shall never desert you and make your enemies triumph over you. Would I not go to hell a million times for you? Would I not like Macbeth's ghost, walk the earth forever for you? Would I not lose the whole world and eternity for you? Would I not cry forever before the footstool of the Lord Omnipotent for you? Would I not die a million deaths for you? Then, why be sad? Cheer up, and be assured that if it takes a million years the sins of our enemies shall visit the millionth generation of those that hinder and oppress us.

Remember that I have sworn by you and my God to serve to the end of all time, the wreck of matter and the crash of worlds. The enemies think that I am defeated. Did the Germans defeat the French in 1870? Did Napoleon really conquer Europe? If so, then I am defeated, but I tell you the world shall hear from my principles even two thousand years hence. I am willing to wait on time for my satisfaction and the retribution of my enemies. Observe my enemies and their children and posterity, and one day you shall see retribution settling around them.

If I die in Atlanta my work shall then only begin, but I shall live, in the physical or spiritual to see the day of Africa's glory. When I am dead wrap the mantle of the Red, Black and Green around me, for in the new life I shall rise with God's grace and blessing to lead the millions up the heights of triumph with the colors that you well know. Look for me in the whirlwind or the storm, look for me all around you, for, with God's grace, I shall come and bring with me countless millions of black slaves who have died in America and the West Indies and the millions in Africa to aid you in the fight for Liberty, Freedom and Life.

The civilization of today is gone drunk and crazy with its power and by such it seeks through injustice, fraud and lies to crush the unfortunate. But if I am apparently crushed by the system of influence and misdirected power, my cause shall rise again to plague the conscience of the corrupt. For this I am satisfied, and for you, I repeat, I am glad to suffer and even die. Again, I say, cheer up, for better days are ahead. I shall write the history that will inspire the millions that are coming and leave the posterity of our enemies to reckon with the hosts for the deeds of their fathers.

With God's dearest blessings, I leave you for awhile.

10
Keeping the Faith[1]

Once back in his native Jamaica, Garvey sought to rebuild his shattered movement and to keep in touch with his still loyal American following. For a time it appeared that he might succeed in reestablishing the Universal Negro Improvement Association as an international force, but the worldwide economic depression of the 1930s ruled out any expensive Negro self-help schemes, and Italy's conquest of Ethiopia was a humiliating reminder of how defenseless was the African motherland. Following an unsuccessful foray into Jamaican politics, in 1935 Garvey moved his headquarters to London, where he published intermittently a monthly magazine of opinion, the Black Man, *until his death in 1940. In 1936, 1937, and 1938 he presided at U.N.I.A. conventions in Toronto, but cut off from direct contact with his dwindling American legions—always his largest base of support—Garvey was helpless to arrest the decline of his once mighty movement. Yet his message remained constant: the importance of African redemption for the benefit of Negroes everywhere, and the central role of American blacks in this endeavor.*

THE AMERICAN NEGRO

There is no doubt that a certain section of the American Negroes are gradually rising in political and economic importance in the country. Their success, however, should be looked at from many points of view, because whatever happens, he is succeeding as a Negro, in the presence of the white man who has always been his original enemy. Not so much that he despises him because he is black, but because he is selfish enough to realize that there may not be enough for both.

During the early days of emancipation, the American Negro was given political privileges in the South, and at that time an observer would think that he had come into a wonderful opportunity that would lead him to his fullest national development by the very fact that he had the rights of the constitution bestowed upon him, and that

[1] From *The Black Man*, November, 1938, pp. 18–19, 20.

period gave the white man the opportunity of studying him, and finding out exclusively what was his aim and ultimate ambition. The
result has been the loss of the vote and the determination to keep him
in the South as a subject race. How well the Southern attitude toward
Negro freedom may be construed in this respect, is left to the opinion
of the student who has gone into the relationships between the two
peoples.

The Universal Negro Improvement Association has always doubted
the genuine sincerity of the white man to entertain the Negro along-
side of him on equal terms, hence we have always fought for the
African nationalism of the race, with the hope of lending the political
support that is necessary not only in America but everywhere else. This
angle of political thought may not be well received by the Negro who
is succeeding to-day, but the student of politics thinks not only of today, but greatly of the to-morrows.

We do hope that the Negro will continue to make all the progress
that is possible to him in America, and that there will be no organized
effort to interfere with such a progress; but whilst we hope for it, we
must also prepare, that if such an interruption comes we will be able
to take care of it. The American Negro occupies a foremost and
prominent position in Negro life. He is the natural leader of all the
Negroes of the world. In his success, he must play the part of leadership, and this must be void of any narrowness as far as the ultimate
and universal progress of the race is concerned. He has been well en-
vironed—buffeted by the highest and best of industrial, commercial
and even political civilization. There is much, therefore, that he can
learn, and the Negro who is succeeding should learn it with sympathy
for those who are not succeeding and with the ultimate idea that whatever knowledge he possesses will be used for the good of all. In all
things he should never forget his race. Any position that he climbs to
must always take with it the relationship of race and what duty can
be performed for the good of that race.

SENATOR BILBO'S BILL

There is to be introduced in the Senate of the United States, in
January of 1939, a very serious Bill, sponsored by Senator Theo. G.
Bilbo of Mississippi, aiming at the repatriation to Africa of as many
of the American Negroes as are desirous of taking advantage of such
privileges under the Bill to be adopted by the United States Government.

The matter of Negro repatriation to Africa has been of continuous
advocacy by the Universal Negro Movement Association, in that the
Association realizes that it is only by the ultimate establishment of

an independent Negro nationality, through which Negro opinion and sentiment can find continuous and uninterrupted expression, may the race hope to hold its own among the competitive races of the world. This view is held irrespective of what our local conditions may happen to be, in the respective communities where we find ourselves, in that local conditions under other people's Governments mean a subjugation of all independent rights, finally relying only on the goodwill and sympathy of other people to treat us as they see fit, which is generally displeasing to us.

Independent nationality is the greatest guarantee of the ability of any people to stand up in our present civilization. Hence the support that the Universal Negro Improvement Association gives to Senator Bilbo, in the respect of this particular Bill, must be considered as something not done because of the man, whatever his previous opinion might have been toward the race, but because of his present attitude in relationship to this Bill that seeks to place the Negro in Africa on a par with any other people in the world.

The Senator's desire for carrying out the purpose of his Bill may not be as idealistic as Negroes may want, but that is not the point to be considered. What is wanted now is the opportunity of the Negro to establish himself, and there is no doubt that this Bill offers such an opportunity. It is hoped, therefore, that no representative and thoughtful group of Negroes in America will oppose the Bill, because they would be opposing the one thing that can ultimately save the Negro from his present condition of helplessness.

Certain American Negroes have had good advantages and privileges in America, and naturally would have no desire to support such a Bill for returning to Africa, but at least these people can realize that the great majority do not share their opinions and views, and would really prefer being in a country of their own. In consideration of these peoples rights, therefore, it is hoped that the privileged and satisfied group will not oppose the Bill. At any rate, it is foolish for the American Negro to put all his eggs in one basket. Whilst some may seriously fight for the realization of the Negro's opportunity in America, another group should fight most strenuously as the Universal Negro Improvement Association is doing, for his complete independence nationally, on the continent of Africa. Let us, therefore, support Senator Bilbo's Bill with the feeling that it strives at a vital question, and one that may be settled without any opposition, if properly considered, either from white or black. All Divisions of the Universal Negro Improvement Association in the United States are therefore asked to give their undivided and wholehearted support to Senator Bilbo's Bill when it is presented in the Senate in January.

THE WORLD LOOKS AT GARVEY

Marcus Garvey's striking ability to reach and hold the loyalty of the black masses was never more apparent than at the early conventions of his Universal Negro Improvement Association. Beginning with the first international gathering of the U.N.I.A., held in New York City throughout the month of August 1920, Garvey astonished the black world with the extent of his following in the United States and abroad, and with the audacity of his program for the economic, political, and spiritual advancement of the race under the red, black, and green banner of Africa. Liberty Hall, the large U.N.I.A. headquarters in Harlem, provided a suitable stage for Garvey to play a variety of roles: the learned educator discoursing on the glories of the Negro past; the visionary provisional president of the Republic of Africa; the triumphant commodore of the Black Star fleet; the fearless commander of the mysterious African Legion; the patron of the new African Orthodox Church. Garvey's sudden rise to prominence, his outspoken criticism of many existing Negro leaders and institutions, and the range and nature of his uplift schemes guaranteed that he would soon be the center of controversy.

11

A New Nation in Harlem[1]

Most contemporary journalists, white and black alike, were inclined to view the pageantry of U.N.I.A. meetings superficially and even cynically, but they were nearly always much impressed by the devotion and enthusiasm of Garveyites. The following balanced account of the second (1921) international convention of the U.N.I.A. recaptures some of the drama and

[1] From Worth Tuttle, "A New Nation in Harlem," *The World Tomorrow,* 4 (September 1921): 279-81.

color, as well as the mood of high expectation, that characterized
the early years of the Garvey movement.

In that section of New York City, beginning approximately at
East 125th Street and continuing to 145th, known as Harlem, and
inhabited almost entirely by negroes, there is a new flag. During this
month of August it is flaunted gaily from the walls of the three buildings which house the offices, industrial exhibit, and second annual
convention of the Universal Negro Improvement Association. It is a
tri-color of red, green and black, the present emblem of the U.N.I.A.,
and the future flag of the Republic of Africa!

Inside Liberty Hall, an immense one-story structure on East 138th
Street where the convention holds its sessions, there is further tangible
evidence of this new nationality. From the ceiling are suspended not
only the flags of the association, but the red, green and black banners
representing the 418 chartered divisions of the Association in the
United States, the West Indies, and Africa. Here, one after another,
an African chieftain, a missionary returned from Abyssinia, a delegate
from Spanish Honduras, an organizer from Louisiana, tell the tales
that are weaving the diverse past and present of the Negro into a
homogeneous future in the U.N.I.A. "In Abyssinia," said the returned
missionary, "I pay a silver dollar bearing a black man's head to a
black station agent for a ticket on a train owned by black men and
manned by a black crew." The crowd applauds and sees an Africa
quite different from the picture it has had of an abode of cannibals.
In a building across the street there is yet more proof of this new unity
in the Women's Industrial Exhibit. There samples of the dress-making,
millinery, and cookery of the American Negro women are displayed
next to the intricate basketry, weaving, and leatherwork of native
African women, and the fancy work and grass-plaiting of the West
Indians.

But it is at the evening meetings of the U.N.I.A., the only one of
the three daily sessions open to the public, that one sees the new nationality in action. Under the banners of South Carolina, Trinidad,
Liberia, sit the delegates from the 840 divisions, chartered and un-
chartered, of the Universal Negro Improvement Association and, to
quote the speakers, "of four hundred million downtrodden Negroes
in the world." While the crowd awaits the parade which precedes the
meeting, ushers sell phonograph records of the Honorable Marcus
Garvey's speeches, and distribute pamphlets advertising shares in the
Black Star Steamship Line and the two million dollar loan for industrial work in Liberia, and *The Mistakes of W. E. B. Du Bois.* The
official band of the Black Star Line plays and the audience sways in

rhythm, drinks pop, and watches the door. The band is suddenly silent, the pop forgotten. . . .

A gowned choir, singing the new anthem of Ethiopia, leads those essentials of a full-grown nation which are illustrated in the nightly procession. There is the head of the future government, the Honorable Marcus Garvey, President-General of the U.N.I.A., in his official robe of red silk and green velvet, surrounded by his statesmen. There is the national army—twelve or more martial figures in attractive blue, red and gold uniforms. There is the corps of Black Cross Nurses and the girl and boy scouts. There is the living symbol of a national life, a black Liberty, draped in red and green, carrying a new scepter, crowned with a black *pileus*. The audience gazes with rapture, thrilled with all the joys of a nationality, without, as yet, any of its responsibilities.

It may be merely an *opera bouffe;* it may be the beginning of all that Mr. Garvey and his followers believe it is. Whatever its future, its present is a vital force in Negro life. Tomorrow Marcus Garvey, hailed in the Harlem newspapers as The Man of the Hour, may be forgotten, but the ideal he has shown and the work he has done thus far toward the attainment of that ideal will not be. He has given the colored peoples the idea of racial self-determination, the blueprint—however vague—of a national home.

If the assumption some of us possess that the exponent of an ideal should be pale, hungry-eyed, worn thin by vigils, is a general one, then Marcus Garvey is a disappointing figure. He is black, apparently too well-fed, exceedingly well groomed. In short, he does not look like —himself. It is when he speaks, whether in the privacy of his office or in the glare of the lights in Liberty Hall, that one recognizes the man for what he is and for what he wants to be, a black leader of black people.

I had attended one meeting in Liberty Hall and had seen the gaudy pageant without having heard Mr. Garvey speak; I had talked with a bumptious employee of the U.N.I.A., and I had passed many doors, in the dingy building occupied by *The Negro World* and the Black Star Line, bearing such inscriptions as High Chancellor and High Commissioner General, before I had an interview with the promoter of it all. Until I met Mr. Garvey, I was a bit supercilious. I found him surprisingly unassuming, even modest, with a very rare use of the perpendicular pronoun. His bearing is that of the educated West Indian Negro, who, neither pathetically humbled nor pathetically arrogated by the burden of prejudice in the United States, meets the white man on his own ground. He is a forceful speaker, with a sincerity in his voice that is convincing. His sentences are short, concise; his words few-syllabled and, for the most part, definite.

When I asked him to explain his plan for the American Negro in regard to Jim Crow cars, disfranchisement, lynching, he answered by explaining the general program of the Universal Negro Improvement Association: Negroes are universally oppressed. Negroes the world over are the victims of prejudice and injustice. Under every government they are unfairly treated, yet are expected to give the same loyalty as other citizens. Here in America during the recent war Negroes contributed money, industrial service, and physical military service, believing that they were helping to make the world safe for a democracy in which they would have a part. Now that the war is over, they are hurled back into the old time status. The Universal Negro Improvement Association believes that petitions and prayers will never help. It believes that Jim Crow cars, disfranchisement, lynching, and burning will prevail so long as Negroes have no united power, no united voice, no economic background to support that voice. Its program is to unite four hundred million Negroes into one solid political body. As Africa is the native habitat of the Negro, from which he was stolen originally, the U.N.I.A. has as its ultimate object the redemption of Africa, where a government of the Negroes, by the Negroes, for the Negroes may be set up. "It may be a matter of centuries," said Mr. Garvey, "before our design can be accomplished, but that is the direction in which we are working."

The present plan for reconquering Africa is by commercial and industrial methods. The Black Star Line has now two passenger and freight vessels operating, more or less regularly, between Africa, the West Indies, and North and South America, and is negotiating for the purchase of the third, the largest of the three. The Association is soliciting subscriptions to a two million dollar loan, at 5 per cent. problematic interest, for the building of schools, factories, and churches in Liberia. On the amount already subscribed a contingent has been sent to Liberia to begin the work. For the present, the efforts of the Association will be confined to Liberia alone; eventually it is hoped to make similar beginnings in other parts of Africa. Mr. Garvey has a plan for the initiation and development of a civil service in which intelligent young men and women in America will be trained for the work in Liberia, and for organization work throughout the world.

Though in his speeches Mr. Garvey seems to be quite openly preparing his subjects for actual combat, he was laconic when I mentioned the military side of the question: "We do not intend to start anything. We are organizing—that's all." In both his speeches and his interviews, he has maintained that he has no enmity for the white peoples. He merely asks for Negroes the same rights and privileges that Caucasians possess. He wants no help from white people in his venture; he scorns organizations of colored people which invite and accept aid from white people. "The Negro race," he said, "must keep to itself socially and politically, while mixing with other races commercially."

I asked Mr. Garvey whether he explained the great popularity of the U.N.I.A. in the West Indies by the fact that he himself is a West Indian and well known in the islands. He admitted that that fact might have some degree of influence, but explained the greater part of the enthusiasm by the condition and environment of the West Indian Negroes. They are more universally educated, more sophisticated politically than the American Negroes. They can understand more readily what a government of their own would mean to them. The American Negro, on the other hand, must be trained to see the advantage in a racial economic and political background.

And here all incongruity between Marcus Garvey, the man, in a calm palm beach suit, and Marcus Garvey, Provisional President of Africa, in a hectic green and red robe, disappeared. Marcus Garvey is out to win his American Negro for the Universal Negro Improvement Association. He knows what bait to use: resounding titles, imperial robes, and a religious ritual. In his dove-tailing of religion and politics, particularly, one sees his skill most clearly. The sessions of the U.N.I.A. are opened with a hymn and a prayer and closed with a benediction. Mr. Garvey's speeches are dotted with references to the Bible and to the American Negro's devotion to religion. He uses the Bible, too, to stir up fighting blood and to pull the wool from the Negro's eyes, if one may judge from a quotation in *The Negro World*: "Negroes heretofore have been accustomed to use the Bible only in solving their problems and, in consequence, have failed, but from now on they will use, in conjunction with the Bible, the material forces and weapons used by the white man in gaining and maintaining his supremacy, in fighting his way to the top."

On "Black Star Night" Mr. Garvey's method of appeal for investment in the steamship line showed that he understands human nature, when it is a matter of getting money, as well as he understands racial traits. He began his appeal by the use of those tricks made familiar to us in the Liberty Loan campaign, such as "five more subscribers before the next number on the program" and "five more who want to hear the band play." His primary address, however, was to the racial consciousness of the audience: "Do you want Africa redeemed? Do you want the Negro respected? Do you want to do your duty by your race? Then buy shares." His second plea was directed at individual self-interest: "Do you want to solve the unemployment situation for Negroes? Do you want jobs as officers and managers instead of cooks and potwashers? Then buy shares." Lastly he reverted to cash return: "This is a little talk on the profitability of speculative investments for the benefit of the hard-headed business men who are not emotionally re-

sponsive to race appeals." He read a list of figures which show that
amounts ranging from $40,000 to $200,000 have been realized on
original investments of one hundred dollars in such stock as the Bell
Telephone, National Cash Register, Underwood Typewriter, and the
like. His statements were punctured by gasps from the audience, but
one wondered whether the gasps came from the hard-headed business
men or from the emotionally inclined, whose early enthusiasm for race
regeneration was being strengthened by the sober second thought of
alluring individual profits! The hard-headed business men know that
these unbelievable returns which Mr. Garvey cited came from speculative ventures, but speculative ventures which had control of monopoly product through patent right, or otherwise, whereas the Black Star
Line is entering competitive shipping at a time when shipping is not
an especially lucrative business. They know that the Black Star Line
must fight its way unaided by monopoly combination, powerful financial connections, or government subsidy.

There is, however, one intangible asset which the steamship line
does possess, the possibility of capitalizing race consciousness. Delegates from Africa affirm that the natives are withholding produce,
awaiting the coming of ships owned and operated by men of their own
color. It may be that Negro shippers of the United States, West Indies,
South America, and Africa will rally to the support of the Black Star
Line, foregoing all considerations but that of race for the time being.
As a debit against this undoubted asset will be the almost assured boycott of the line by white shippers. Probably the gains of race consciousness will offset the losses, but the point is that even a mildly profitable
oceanic trade, say five per cent. net to the stockholders, will not be
achieved within a short enough time to appeal to the hard-headed
business men. In fact, the promise of cash return on Black Star stock
may be the undoing of the entire movement.

To judge from the present temper of the members of the U.N.I.A.,
ruin due to such a cause would be pathetic. Mr. Garvey and his officials
have openly acknowledged that thus far the undertaking has not paid
and in defense have pointed to the common fallibility of man, including J. P. Morgan. Their supporters have accepted their defense and
reassured them of their confidence and their faith. Or, as one woman
delegate from Pittsburg philosophically expressed it in a stirring speech
before the convention: "Even if Garvey should run away with all the
money, we'd rather he did it than to have some white man lose it for
us."

It would seem from all observations that Mr. Garvey *has* won the
American Negro, at least the members of the Universal Negro Improve-
ment Association, to the support of his idea. They look upon the Black
Star Line and the African Communities League in the way Mr. Garvey

would have them look on it—as agents of racial regeneration rather than as agents of monetary return. It would seem that the wise policy for the directors would be to stop talking about fabulous returns and to admit the impossibility of dividends for a long time to come. Otherwise the clamor of disappointed investors may stifle the voice of an awakening people.

12

DuBois Asks Some Searching Questions[1]

Garvey's very success, especially his ability to raise large sums of money for the Black Star Line and other U.N.I.A. ventures, was soon generating not only admiration from his followers but also concern and opposition from some other Negro leaders. Part of the criticism could be dismissed as simple jealousy of this young West Indian who had captured a larger following in a few short years than had any previous American black spokesman or organization. Some of the skeptics were genuinely fearful, however, that Garvey was leading the black masses astray, and that he lacked the administrative experience and skill to make his daring dreams a reality. His failure, they felt, would mean not only financial loss and heartache to many poor blacks but also a damaging setback to the cause of Negro unity. One of Garvey's earliest and most persistent critics was Dr. W. E. Burghardt DuBois, the scholarly editor of Crisis, *the organ of the National Association for the Advancement of Colored People. DuBois's opposition became increasingly vehement as he learned more about the mismanagement of various U.N.I.A. enterprises. As early as December 1920, while Garvey was still very much the hero of the black world, DuBois offered his first tentative criticism in a two-part article in* Crisis.

Marcus Garvey was born at St. Ann's Bay, Jamaica, about 1885. He was educated at the public school and then for a short time attended the Church of England Grammar School, although he was a Roman Catholic by religion. On leaving school he learned the printing trade and followed it for many years. In Costa Rica he was associated with Marclam Taylor in publishing the *Bluefield's Messenger.* Later he was on the staff of *La Nacion.* He then returned to Jamaica and worked as a printer, being foreman of the printing department of

[1] From W. E. B. DuBois, "Marcus Garvey," *Crisis* 21 (December 1920, January 1921): 58–60, 112–15. Reprinted by permission of *The Crisis* Magazine.

P. Benjamin's Manufacturing Company of Kingston. Later he visited Europe and spent some time in England and France and while abroad conceived his scheme of organizing the Negro Improvement Society. This society was launched August 1, 1914, in Jamaica, with these general objects among others:

"To establish a Universal Confraternity among the race"; "to promote the spirit of race pride and love"; "to administer to and assist the needy"; "to strengthen the imperialism of independent African States"; "to conduct a world-wide commercial and industrial intercourse".

His first practical object was to be the establishment of a farm school. Meetings were held and the Roman Catholic Bishop, the Mayor of Kingston, and many others addressed them. Nevertheless the project did not succeed and Mr. Garvey was soon in financial difficulties. He therefore practically abandoned the Jamaica field and came to the United States. In the United States his movement for many years languished until at last with the increased migration from the West Indies during the war he succeeded in establishing a strong nucleus in the Harlem district of New York City.

His program now enlarged and changed somewhat in emphasis. He began especially to emphasize the commercial development of the Negroes and as an islander familiar with the necessities of ship traffic he planned the "Black Star Line". The public for a long time regarded this as simply a scheme of exploitation, when they were startled by hearing that Garvey had bought a ship. This boat was a former coasting vessel, 32 years old, but it was put into commission with a black crew and a black captain and was announced as the first of a fleet of vessels which would trade between the colored peoples of America, the West Indies and Africa. With this beginning, the popularity and reputation of Mr. Garvey and his association increased quickly.

In addition to the *Yarmouth* he is said to have purchased two small boats, the *Shadyside,* a small excursion steamer which made daily excursions up the Hudson, and a yacht which was designed to cruise among the West Indies and collect cargo in some central spot for the *Yarmouth.* He had first announced the Black Star Line as a Five Million Dollar corporation, but in February, 1920, he announced that it was going to be a Ten Million Dollar corporation with shares selling at Five Dollars. To this he added in a few months the Negro Factories Corporation capitalized at One Million Dollars with two hundred thousand one dollar shares, and finally he announced the subscription of Five Million Dollars to free Liberia and Haiti from debt.

Early in 1920 he called a convention of Negroes to meet in New York City from the 1st to the 31st of August, "to outline a constructive plan and program for the uplifting of the Negroes and the redemption of

Africa". He also took title to three apartment houses to be used as offices and purchased the foundation of an unfinished Baptist church which he covered over and used for meetings, calling it "Liberty Hall". In August, 1920, his convention met with representatives from various parts of the United States, several of the West India Islands and the Canal Zone and a few from Africa. The convention carried out its plan of a month's meetings and culminated with a mass meeting which filled Madison Square Garden. Finally the convention adopted a "Declaration of Independence" with 66 articles, a universal anthem and colors,—red, black and green—and elected Mr. Garvey as "His Excellency, the Provisional President of Africa", together with a number of various other leaders from the various parts of the Negro world. This in brief is the history of the Garvey movement.

The question comes (1) Is it an honest sincere movement? (2) Are its industrial and commercial projects business like and effective? (3) Are its general objects plausible and capable of being carried out?

The central and dynamic force of the movement is Garvey. He has with singular success capitalized and made vocal the great and long suffering grievances and spirit of protest among the West Indian peasantry. Hitherto the black peasantry of the West Indies has been almost leaderless. Its natural leaders, both mulatto and black, have crossed the color line and practically obliterated social distinction and to some extent economic distinction, between them and the white English world on the Islands. This has left a peasantry with only the rudiments of education and with almost no economic chances, grovelling at the bottom. Their distress and needs gave Garvey his vision.

It is a little difficult to characterize the man Garvey. He has been charged with dishonesty and graft, but he seems to me essentially an honest and sincere man with a tremendous vision, great dynamic force, stubborn determination and unselfish desire to serve; but also he has very serious defects of temperament and training; he is dictatorial, domineering, inordinately vain and very suspicious. He cannot get on with his fellow-workers. His entourage has continually changed. He has had endless law suits and some cases of fisticuffs with his subordinates and has even divorced the young wife whom he married with great fanfare of trumpets about a year ago. All these things militate against him and his reputation. Nevertheless I have not found the slightest proof that his objects were not sincere or that he was consciously diverting money to his own uses. The great difficulty with him is that he has absolutely no business sense, no *flair* for real organization and his general objects are so shot through with bombast and exaggeration that it is difficult to pin them down for careful examination.

On the other hand, Garvey is an extraordinary leader of men. Thousands of people believe in him. He is able to stir them with singular eloquence and the general run of his thought is of a high plane. He has become to thousands of people a sort of religion. He allows and encourages all sorts of personal adulation, even printing in his paper the addresses of some of the delegates who hailed him as "His Majesty". He dons on state occasion, a costume consisting of an academic cap and gown flounced in red and green!

Of Garvey's curious credulity and suspicions one example will suffice: In March, 1919, he held a large mass meeting at Palace Casino which was presided over by Chandler Owen and addressed by himself and Phillip Randolph. Here he collected $204 in contributions on the plea that while in France, W. E. B. DuBois had interfered with the work of his "High Commissioner" by "defeating" his articles in the French press and "repudiating" his statements as to lynching and injustice in America! The truth was that Mr. DuBois never saw or heard of his "High Commissioner", never denied his nor anyone's statements of the wretched American conditions, did everything possible to arouse rather than quiet the French press and would have been delighted to welcome and co-operate with any colored fellow-worker.

When it comes to Mr. Garvey's industrial and commercial enterprises there is more ground for doubt and misgiving than in the matter of his character. First of all, his enterprises are incorporated in Delaware, where the corporation laws are loose and where no financial statements are required. So far as I can find, and I have searched with care, Mr. Garvey has never published a complete statement of the income and expenditures of the Negro Improvement Association or of the Black Star Line or of any of his enterprises, which really revealed his financial situation. A courteous letter of inquiry sent to him July 22, 1920, asking for such financial data as he was willing for the public to know, remains to this day unacknowledged and unanswered.

Now a refusal to publish a financial statement is no proof of dishonesty, but it *is* proof that either Garvey is ill-advised and unnecessarily courting suspicion, or that his industrial enterprises are not on a sound business basis; otherwise he is too good an advertiser not to use a promising balance-sheet for all it is worth.

There has been one balance sheet, published July 26, 1920, purporting to give the financial condition of the Black Star Line after one year of operation; neither profit or loss is shown, there is no way to tell the actual cash receipts or the true condition of the business. Nevertheless it does make some interesting revelations.

The total amount of stock subscribed for is $590,860. Of this $118,-153.28 is not yet paid for, leaving the actual amount of paid-in capital charged against the corporation, $472,706.72. Against this stands only

$355,214.59 of assets (viz.: $21,985.21 in cash deposits and loans receivable; $12,975.01 in furniture and equipment, $288,515.37 which is the alleged value of his boats, $26,000 in real estate and $5,739 of insurance paid in advance). To offset the assets he has $152,264.14 of other liabilities (accrued salaries, $1,539.30; notes and accounts payable, $129,224.84; mortgages due, $21,500). In other words, his capital stock of $472,706.72 is after a year's business impaired to such extent that he has only $202,950.45 to show for it.

Even this does not reveal the precariousness of his actual business condition. Banks before the war in lending their credit refused to recognize any business as safe unless for every dollar of current liabilities there were *two* dollars of current assets. Today, since the war, they require *three* dollars of current assets to every *one* of current liabilities. The Black Star Line had July 26, $16,485.21 in current assets and $130,764.14 in current liabilities, when recognition by any reputable bank called for $390,000 in current assets.

Moreover, another sinister admission appears in this statement: the cost of floating the Black Star Line to date has been $289,066.27. In other words, it has cost nearly $300,000 to collect a capital of less than half a million. Garvey has, in other words, spent more for advertisement than he has for his boats!

This is a serious situation, and even this does not tell the whole story: the real estate, furniture, etc., listed above, are probably valued correctly. But how about the boats? The *Yarmouth* is a wooden steamer of 1,452 gross tons, built in 1887. It is old and unseaworthy; it came near sinking a year ago and it has cost a great deal for repairs. It is said that it is now laid up for repairs with a large bill due. Without doubt the inexperienced purchasers of this vessel paid far more than it is worth, and it will soon be utterly worthless unless rebuilt at a very high cost.

The cases of the *Kanawha* (or *Antonio Maceo*) and the *Shadyside* are puzzling. Neither of these boats is registered as belonging to the Black Star Line at all. The former is recorded as belonging to C. L. Dimon, and the latter to the North and East River Steamboat Company. Does the Black Star Line really own these boats, or is it buying them by installments, or only leasing them? We do not know the facts and have been unable to find out. Under the circumstances they look like dubious "assets".

The majority of the Black Star Stock is apparently owned by the Universal Negro Improvement Association. There is no reason why this association, if it will and can, should not continue to pour money into its corporation. Let us therefore consider then Mr. Garvey's other resources.

Mr. Garvey's income consists of (a) dues from members of the

U. N. I. Association; (b) shares in the Black Star Line and other enter-prises, and (c) gifts and "loans" for specific objects. If the U. N. I. Association has "3,000,000 members" then the income from that source alone would be certainly over a million dollars a year. If, as is more likely, it has under 300,000 paying members, he may collect $150,000 annually from this source. Stock in the Black Star Line is still being sold. Garvey himself tells of one woman who had saved about four hundred dollars in gold: "She brought out all the gold and bought shares in the Black Star Line." Another man writes this touching letter from the Canal Zone: "I have sent twice to buy shares amounting to $125, (numbers of certificates 3752 and 9617). Now I am sending $35 for seven more shares. You might think I have money, but the truth, as I stated before, is that I have no money now. But if I'm to die of hunger it will be all right because I'm determined to do all that's in my power to better the conditions of my race."

In addition to this he has asked for special contributions. In the spring of 1920 he demanded for his coming convention in August, "a fund of two million dollars ($2,000,000) to capitalize this, the great-est of all conventions." In October he acknowledged a total of some-thing over $16,000 in small contributions. Immediately he announced "a constructive loan" of $2,000,000, which he is presumably still seek-ing to raise.

From these sources of income Mr. Garvey has financed his enter-prises and carried on a wide and determined propaganda, maintained a large staff of salaried officials, clerks and agents, and published a weekly newspaper. Nothwithstanding this considerable income, there is no doubt that Garvey's expenditures are pressing hard on his in-come, and that his financial methods are so essentially unsound that unless he speedily revises them the investors will certainly get no divi-dends and worse may happen. He is apparently using the familiar method of "Kiting"—i.e., the money which comes in as investment in stock is being used in current expenses, especially in heavy overhead costs, for clerk hire, interest and display. Even his boats are being used for advertisement more than for business—lying in harbors as exhibits, taking excursion parties, etc. These methods have necessi-tated mortgages on property and continually new and more grandiose schemes to collect larger and larger amounts of ready cash. Meantime, lacking business men of experience, his actual business ventures have brought in few returns, involved heavy expense and threatened him continually with disaster or legal complication.

On the other hand, full credit must be given Garvey for a bold effort and some success. He has at least put vessels manned and owned by black men on the seas and they have carried passengers and cargoes. The difficulty is that he does not know the shipping business, he does not understand the investment of capital, and he has few trained and staunch assistants.

The present financial plight of an inexperienced and headstrong promoter may therefore decide the fate of the whole movement. This would be a calamity. Garvey is the beloved leader of tens of thousands of poor and bewildered people who have been cheated all their lives. His failure would mean a blow to their faith, and a loss of their little savings, which it would take generations to undo.

Moreover, shorn of its bombast and exaggeration, the main lines of the Garvey plan are perfectly feasible. What he is trying to say and do is this: American Negroes can, by accumulating and ministering their own capital, organize industry, join the black centers of the south Atlantic by commercial enterprise and in this way ultimately redeem Africa as a fit and free home for black men. This is true. It is *feasible*. It is, in a sense, practical; but it will take for its accomplishment long years of painstaking, self-sacrificing effort. It will call for every ounce of ability, knowledge, experience and devotion in the whole Negro race. It is not a task for one man or one organization, but for co-ordinate effort on the part of millions. The plan is not original with Garvey but he has popularized it, made it a living, vocal ideal and swept thousands with him with intense belief in the possible accomplishment of the ideal.

This is a great, human service; but when Garvey forges ahead and almost single-handed attempts to realize his dream in a few years, with large words and wild gestures, he grievously minimizes his task and endangers his cause.

To instance one illustrative fact: there is no doubt but what Garvey has sought to import to America and capitalize the antagonism between blacks and mulattoes in the West Indies. This has been the cause of the West Indian failures to gain headway against the whites. Yet Garvey imports it into a land where it has never had any substantial footing and where today, of all days, it is absolutely repudiated by every thinking Negro; Garvey capitalizes it, has sought to get the coöperation of men like R. R. Moton on this basis, and has aroused more bitter color enmity inside the race than has ever before existed. The whites are delighted at the prospect of a division of our solidifying phalanx, but their hopes are vain. American Negroes recognize no color line in or out of the race, and they will in the end punish the man who attempts to establish it.

Then too Garvey increases his difficulties in other directions. He is a British subject. He wants to trade in British territory. Why then does he needlessly antagonize and even insult Britain? He wants to unite all Negroes. Why then does he sneer at the work of the powerful group of his race in the United States where he finds asylum and sympathy? Particularly, why does he decry the excellent and rising business enterprises of Harlem—intimating that his schemes alone are honest and sound when the facts flatly contradict him? He proposes to settle his headquarters in Liberia—but has he asked permission of the Liberian government? Does he presume to usurp authority in a land which has successfully withstood England, France and the United States,—but is expected tamely to submit to Marcus Garvey? How long does Mr. Garvey think that President King would permit his anti-English propaganda on Liberian soil, when the government is straining every nerve to escape the Lion's Paw?

And, finally, without arms, money, effective organization or base of operations, Mr. Garvey openly and wildly talks of "Conquest" and of telling white Europeans in Africa to "get out!" and of becoming himself a black Napoleon!

Suppose Mr. Garvey should drop from the clouds and concentrate on his industrial schemes as a practical first step toward his dreams: the first duty of a great commercial enterprise is to carry on effective commerce. A man who sees in industry the key to a situation, must establish sufficient business-like industries. Here Mr. Garvey has failed lamentably.

The *Yarmouth*, for instance, has not been a commercial success. Stories have been published alleging its dirty condition and the inexcusable conduct of its captain and crew. To this Mr. Garvey may reply that it was no easy matter to get efficient persons to run his boats and to keep a schedule. This is certainly true, but if it is difficult to secure one black boat crew, how much more difficult is it going to be to "build and operate factories in the big industrial centers of the United States, Central America, the West Indies and Africa to manufacture every marketable commodity"? and also "to purchase and build ships of larger tonnage for the African and South American trade"? and also to raise "Five Million Dollars to free Liberia" where "new buildings are to be erected, administrative buildings are to be built, colleges and universities are to be constructed"? and finally to accomplish what Mr. Garvey calls the "Conquest of Africa"!

To sum up: Garvey is a sincere, hard-working idealist; he is also a stubborn, domineering leader of the mass; he has worthy industrial and commercial schemes but he is an inexperienced business man. His dreams of Negro industry, commerce and the ultimate freedom of Africa are feasible; but his methods are bombastic, wasteful, illogical and ineffective and almost illegal. If he learns by experience, attracts strong and capable friends and helpers instead of making needless enemies; if he gives up secrecy and suspicion and substitutes open and frank reports as to his income and expenses, and above all if he is willing to be a co-worker and not a czar, he may yet in time succeed in at least starting some of his schemes toward accomplishment. But unless he does these things and does them quickly he cannot escape failure.

Let the followers of Mr. Garvey insist that he get down to bed-rock business and make income and expense balance: let them gag Garvey's wilder words, and still preserve his wide power and influence. American Negro leaders are not jealous of Garvey—they are not envious of his success; they are simply afraid of his failure, for his failure would be theirs. He can have all the power and money that he can efficiently and honestly use, and if in addition he wants to prance down Broadway in a green shirt, let him—but do not let him foolishly overwhelm with bankruptcy and disaster one of the most interesting spiritual movements of the modern Negro world.

13
Garvey's Message
Reaches Africa[1]

Ironically, the first provisional president of the Republic of Africa was destined never to set foot on African soil. Yet Garvey's call for the liberation of the motherland quickly reached the remotest parts of Africa, inspiring many native blacks with hope for their ultimate independence from European colonial rule. A number of African delegates attended the first U.N.I.A. convention in 1920 and helped to draft the Declaration of Rights of the Negro Peoples of the World, and the Garvey movement initially received strong support from some officials of the Liberian government. The extent of this African interest in Garveyism, even in the remote back country, was still vivid in the memory of a British colonial officer writing in World War II about his experiences in Nigeria two decades earlier.

Somewhere down the Niger valley, twenty years ago, a horse boy was arrested by the local Emir, and sent to my camp for talking sedition. He had been telling the local pagans, wild islanders, that a black king was coming, with a great iron ship full of black soldiers, to drive all the whites out of Africa. The Emir suggested that he ought to be flogged and deported.

My political agent, Musa, an old Hausa from the north, said that the village markets were full of this talk and asked if there were any truth in it. I told him that it was nonsense. But he looked unconvinced and said doubtfully, "A steamship, they say, sir, a white man's ship, but with black officers and a black crew."

"How could that be, Musa? It's only village talk."

Musa was a professional diplomat and agent, of a kind no longer known in Europe, without a nation of his own. He offered his gifts, as negotiator and adviser on local affairs, as gauger of local feeling, to the highest bidder. He had belonged to two Emir's courts before

[1] From Joyce Cary, *The Case for African Freedom* (Austin: University of Texas Press, 1962), pp. 19–22. Reprinted by permission of the University of Texas Press.

he came to me. He seemed to be as far removed from racial prejudice or nationalist feeling as any dog-fancier who is called in to manage an international show. He was a cosmopolitan, cool, well-mannered, extremely shrewd, and rather lazy-minded. His feelings were shallow. But the notion of a ship with black officers and crew, coming across the ocean, moved him to some deep and private excitement. He was unwilling to believe that such a ship did not exist.

The horse boy denied the story and I advised the Emir to let him go. It was not for many years afterwards that I heard of the Black Star Steamship Company and its founder, Marcus Garvey, provisional President of Africa.

I don't suppose any of my colleagues heard of him sooner, if at all. Marcus Garvey was a negro who held a congress in New York and drew up a Declaration of Rights for the negro peoples of the world. He also founded the Steamship Company, to be under negro control, and to trade with Africa.

Garvey's representatives were deported from Liberia, and chased out of the Belgian Congo. The Governor of Sierra Leone congratulated President King of Liberia on "showing the door to spurious patriots from across the Atlantic, men who sought to make Liberia a focus for racial animosity."

The ship company failed, and there were bitter quarrels among the directors. The whole episode, at least in the white newspapers, cut a comic figure. Yet Garvey's manifesto went all through Africa. I cannot be sure, of course, that the story which came to my remote district, four days' journey from a telegraph office and eight from a railway, was about Garvey and his ship. I thought it nonsense, asked for no particulars, and I don't remember its date. I was like the other whites. I knew nothing of what was going on in the native mind. Seeing primitive people in their isolated villages, I assumed that their ideas of the world were primitive, that they were isolated also in mind.

But they were not. In a continent still illiterate, where all news goes by mouth and every man is a gatherer, news of any incident affecting the relations of black and white, a strike in South Africa, war with Abyssinia, spreads through the whole country in a few weeks. It is the most exciting of news; above all, if it tells, of a black victory.

To Musa, I suppose, with his education, his cynical pessimism, the black steamship appeared like a startling triumph. He thought nothing of manifestos or the rights of peoples, but he was clever enough to set great value on economic power, and the control of expensive machinery. He had not expected to hear of black men owning and driving ocean-going ships, and he was deeply moved. He felt his colour.

This is a root fact of African politics: colour, race.

Garvey's Declaration told of the workings of the colour bar:

"Nowhere in the world with few exceptions are black men accorded equal treatment with white men but are discriminated against for no other reason than their race and colour.

"Against such inhuman and un-Christian and uncivilized treatment we protest and invoke the condemnation of all mankind.

"We believe in the freedom of Africa for the negro people of the world; we demand Africa for the Africans."

Garvey was a Jamaican, and, as Africans pointed out, he did not represent Africa. But only officials completely cut off by office work from political reality could fail to know that his declaration represented two things far more powerful than votes: a racial grievance and the moral sense of humanity. These spring from entirely different roots but they are two of the most powerful political forces in the world. They never cease their growth and pressure.

It was not votes that abolished the slave trade. It was a few enthusiasts, despised and politically impotent, Quakers, poets, appealing only to moral force, who began that agitation, which, in the end, cost the British parliament twenty million pounds, and the U.S.A. a civil war and nearly a million dead.

The British government was wise, even at a time of national poverty, after the Napoleonic war, to spend some millions on freeing the slaves. It saved itself from far greater expense and incalculable misfortune.

Garvey's movement effected nothing at that time, but it would be great folly for any European government, with African dependencies, to forget it, or to forget the realities of its position in Africa. It may be one of the better colonizing powers, honestly seeking the welfare of its subjects. But it stands before the world as a defendant. It has to answer a charge. "What are you doing in Africa? What are you getting out of it? What does the African gain by your rule? Have you a colour bar?"

This is the moral question. It may be said that though public opinion always acts upon a moral impulse, it takes often a long time to gather momentum. Official contempt of Garvey's movement, and a great many others of the same kind, is based upon the secret reflection, "Things will last for my time." But will they?

14

British and French Apprehension[1]

The Garvey movement was clearly a threat to the stability of European colonial rule in Africa, and the British and French governments reacted accordingly. Their pressure was undoubtedly one of the major reasons that the government of Liberia, the only independent black state in Africa at the time, abruptly canceled its permission for a U.N.I.A. settlement at Cape Palmas in 1924 and deported the advance party of Garveyites. The extent of British and French concern over the Garvey movement's appeal for their African subjects is reflected in the following dispatch from the British Consul General in Dakar, French West Africa, to Lord Curzon, the Foreign Secretary, in the summer of 1922.

TO LORD CURZON

British Consulate-General
Dakar, 17th August, 1922.

My Lord:

For some considerable time past, the French Authorities here have been engaged in watching with some uneasiness the activities of a group of men, for the most part natives of Sierra Leone, who were believed to be the local representatives of an American Association directed by negroes [sic] called the UNIVERSAL NEGRO IMPROVEMENT SOCIETY, which has at its head the notorious Marcus Garvey, the self-styled apostle of negro emancipation, and President of the "Negro Republic of Africa."

In due course domiciliary perquisitions at the dwellings of some of these men were instituted by the police, resulting in the seizure of a large dossier of documents which shewed clearly that the persons in whose possession they were found were acting as the representatives of the Association named, and distributing broadcast its propaganda; fur-

[1] From *Science and Society*, Summer, 1968, pp. 322–23.

92

ther, that at Dakar, Rufisque, and Thiès active branches, provided with the usual staff of elected officers had been established, which branches were likewise engaged in spreading the objects of the parent body, and in collecting subscriptions for the furtherance of its schemes.

Among the documents seized were several relating to the visit, in the month of May last, of a delegate from the United States named JOHN KAMARA, who was described as the Society's "Travelling Commissioner." In this person's honour meetings were held in the various established centres which were addressed by him in violent language exhorting his hearers by all means to spread the revolutionary movement which would, in the end, cast the white man out of Africa, and much more to the same effect. "Appropriate" replies, of which verbatim records were discovered, couched in similar language, were made by the local heads. From Dakar KAMARA left for the Gambia, his intention being to proceed to all the West African Divisions in turn.

Following these seizures, four men, natives of Sierra Leone, named WILSON, FARMER, DOHERTY, and BROWN, were recently deported by Arrêté of the Governor-General to their native Colony, for taking part in the activities of the Universal Negro Improvement Society, which the French Administration have always regarded as seditious and antieuropean; whilst many more have been warned by the police. Special observation is being kept on any known to have had copies of the "Negro World," the organ of the Society, in their possession, that journal having been prohibited in the French Colonies under penalty.

In the British Colonies in West Africa, however, the Universal Negro Improvement Society, whilst strongly appealing to the imagination of the natives, who, in certain of them, are said to have embraced its objects with enthusiasm, would not appear to be regarded by the respective Governments with the same uneasiness as it has awakened in the French Divisions; one is informed that in British West Africa it is permitted freely to develop its activities, and there to enroll immense numbers of adherents to a movement which is said to have for its object nothing short of "Africa for the African."

The curious spectacle is thus afforded of the existence of a movement presumably of an anti-european character, originating among negroes in the United States, sternly repressed in eleven French Colonies, and indulgently tolerated in four British Divisions. I have duly informed the Governors of the Gambia, Sierra Leone, Gold Coast, and Nigeria of what has taken place, and I now consider it to be my duty to report the matter to your Lordship as well.

I have, etc.
(Sgd.) R. C. F. Maugham,
His Majesty's Consul-General.

15
African Suspicion[1]

Not all black Africans reacted favorably to the Garvey movement. While applauding the interest in African liberation by Negroes in the United States and elsewhere in the New World, some Africans considered Garvey's views on Africa simplistic and his program ill conceived. One such critic was M. Mokete Manoedi, a young African studying in the United States—the son of a warrior chief in Basutoland, South Africa—who went to considerable effort to warn American Negroes of his suspicion of Garvey's intentions.

The American people are unfortunately misled into believing that the theatrical blandishments and grandiose preachments and threats of Mr. Garvey have some prospects of enlisting the sympathy and support of native Africans. This idea is artfully cultivated and nurtured by Mr. Garvey and his cohorts by spreading broadcast erroneous reports to the effect that native Africans will represent my people in the coming so-called Third International Congress. Upon this specious and false claim, the U. N. I. A. hopes to separate the poor, well-meaning, but misguided and ignorant Negroes from their hard earnings. It is against this wanton and unscrupulous betrayal of the interests, hopes and rights of my people that I have decided to raise my voice. African Chiefs have no interest in the Garvey Movement and would not think of establishing relations with it.

He is a megalomaniac conferring titles upon greedy recipients here in New York. He has created a Sir Ferris, a Sir Bruce, a Lady Davis here. He is expecting a crown for himself, from their hands in Africa.

It might be interesting to the American people to know that the native African is not too backward and stupid to see through the sham, hypocrisy, and demagogy of these shouters about redeeming Africa.

It may not be amiss also to state who I am. It very naturally occurs

[1] From M. Mokete Manoedi, *Garvey and Africa* (New York: New York Age Press [1922?]), pp. 3–4.

to the mind of the intelligent reader to interrogate, by what authority do you speak?

I was born in the territory of Leribe, Basutoland, South Africa, under the tribal rule of Chief Jonothan Malapo Mosheshe, and the reign of the Paramount Chief Letsie Mosheshe. My father was Chief Manoedi of the Molibeli people, and he was known throughout the Basutoland as a warrior and statesman. I was placed very early under the tutelage of the Paramount Chief Letsie, for the usual purpose of becoming familiar (as the son of a Chief) with the customs and usages of the Lekhotla (Court). I came to maturity thoroughly experienced in their ways and the art of War, thoroughly acquainted with the mind of my own and neighboring peoples'. I have observed that those who talk of redeeming Africa, sense it in terms of ruling Africa. They seem wholly uninitiated into the mysteries of the African psychology. There is an African Will, and I advise somebody, who is not asking my advice, to become acquainted with it, before attempting to set up a throne in Africa. I am reminded here of the Basuto tradition apropos the association of this people with the British Government. It is not secret history, that while the white man conquered and rules the resources of Africa he found it not unimportant to placate and court the favor of its all-powerful chiefs. I wish to remind Garvey here, who has emphasized his own and other peoples' blackness, that even so he is not sufficiently African as to be undiscovered amongst them.

Granted African emancipation possible there, it has been set back for some time by Garvey's misdirected zeal. Suspicion has fallen upon the great black world and the conqueror will the more guard with redoubtable barriers of steel. All unredeemed peoples must be redeemed through the cooperation of all races.

My people are not favorably impressed either with the unmitigated presumption of this man in electing himself Provisional-President of Africa. They want to know the source of his right. Besides, how inconsistent are his practices and professions. Think, if you will, of a Provisional-President of a Republic Knighting Citizens! Only Kings and Emperors confer titles upon subjects. A Republic is supposed to rest upon a citizen-ship-equality. But I suppose this small matter of political-civics has no weight with this self-styled saviour of the African people.

In the coming Convention it would be interesting to request Mr. Garvey to indicate the tribes that have sent Africans to America to represent them. It is very significant that President King of the Republic of Liberia, while in this country, would have absolutely nothing to do with Mr. Garvey and his movement, although a so-called

Liberian Redemption Loan was advertised as being raised by the Garvey Movement.

I love my people. I want to see them educated, developed and grow in power for they represent a great race.

Such is my reason for presenting this little pamphlet to the non-African world—white, yellow, brown and black.

16

An Answer to Garvey's Appeal to White America[1]

Because Garvey believed that all men should be proud of their race, he admired whites who openly championed racial purity and the social separation of the races in America. He considered them far less hypocritical than the white backers of the N.A.A.C.P., who professed to believe in integration and equal rights for Negroes. This thoroughly racist view of American society led Garvey into a strange flirtation with the Ku Klux Klan and other white-supremacy groups whose stand against race-mixing paralleled that of the U.N.I.A. Such contacts with white extremists were denounced by other Negro leaders as a betrayal, of course, but Garvey merely labeled his critics amalgamationists and mongrelizers. One of his white backers was John Powell of the Anglo-Saxon Clubs of America, a white-supremacy organization based in Richmond, Virginia. Shortly after Garvey's imprisonment in 1925, Powell assured the U.N.I.A. membership in a speech at Liberty Hall that they could count on the support of Southern whites in their efforts to secure the release of their martyred leader.

Mr. Chairman and members of the Universal Negro Improvement Association, I have never in my life been more touched and more moved, than by the cordial reception you have given me and my friends tonight. I wish I were an orator so that I might give adequate expression to the feelings and the thoughts that are moving in me.

I would like to tell you how it was that I came to know more about your organization, and the purposes for which it stands. Major Ernest Sevier Cox, a man who spent six years of his life traveling all around the world in order to study racial problems in various parts of the world, wrote a book called "White America." Major Cox was for sev-

[1] From Amy Jacques Garvey, ed., *Philosophy and Opinions of Marcus Garvey*, vol. II (New York: Universal Publishing House, 1926), pp. 339–41, 342–43, 346–47, 349. Reprinted by permission of Amy Jacques Garvey.

eral years in Africa; he worked in the mines in South Africa; he went
through the whole length and breadth of Africa from the Cape up to
Cairo, studying the various problems that came under his observation.
He wrote this book, "White America," the purpose of which was to
find a real and ultimate solution to that great problem which has
vexed the mind and heart of all America now for 200 years and
more. His book was very violently criticised by certain newspapers
which I believe, are under the influence of the National Association
for the Advancement of Colored People. So it was a great surprise as
well as a great pleasure to Major Cox when he received a letter from
a member of the Garvey organization in St. Louis. His letter told
Major Cox that its writer had seen a copy of "White America," had
read it and felt tremendously encouraged to find that there was a
white man advocating essentially the cause of the Garvey movement.
He wrote that there were many things in that book which he could
not approve of, as his point of view was different, but it was a great
joy to the members of that Chapter of the Universal Negro Improvement Association to find that there was a white man who was seriously
advocating those very purposes for which Marcus Garvey stood.

MAJOR COX'S LETTER

He requested Major Cox to write a letter to be read before that
branch of your organization. Major Cox wrote a very strong and very
moving letter, which was read by Mr. Ditto before his organization,
and he wrote back to Major Cox and said, "I wish you could have
been here to have seen the enthusiasm with which your letter was
received; our members are reading and studying "White America,"
and many of the members have said that "White America" should
be in every Negro's home along with the Bible." Major Cox was naturally very pleased with this, and later when Mr. Ditto asked if he
might publish the letter Major Cox suggested that he enlarge on the
letter. The result of that was a little pamphlet which Mr. Cox wrote
and published, entitled "Let My People Go." It is a message from
white men who wish to keep the white race white to black men who
wish to keep the black race black; and it is dedicated to Marcus Garvey, that great leader who has sought to do for his own race what the
greatest of white Americans sought to do for that race and to encourage the race to do for itself—none other than Abraham Lincoln.

WITH MARCUS GARVEY AT ATLANTA

This pamphlet was brought to the attention of your great leader
and he corresponded with Major Cox, and last June when I went

down to Georgia to address the Georgia Legislature in favor of a bill for the preservation of racial integrity, I went to the prison to see Marcus Garvey. I expected to see a man with bowed head; I expected to see a man depressed and unhappy and embittered, because in the meantime I had read his "Appeal to the Soul of White America," and it had touched me to the heart. When I saw him I saw a man with head erect, with eyes open and clear, unashamed and unafraid, free from all bitterness, free of rancor; not one word of complaint escaped his lips, not one word of bemoaning; his one thought was for you— his people and his loyal followers. And as we discussed these matters I found that in every essential principle the ideals and ideas of Marcus Garvey were identical with those of the organization which I have the honor to represent—the Anglo-Saxon Clubs of America.

There was nothing that Marcus Garvey could not say frankly and freely to me without danger of misunderstanding; there was nothing that I could not say to Marcus Garvey openly and frankly and freely without danger of misunderstanding; and I realized that I was in the presence of a man of the highest idealism and the noblest courage and the profoundest wisdom; a man dedicated to a noble and a sacred cause—the cause of the independence and integrity of his race. . . .

THE NEGRO IS AWAKE

One more thing: A member of your organization in Detroit got in touch with Major Cox and asked him to send out 50 copies of "White America." Major Cox sent the copies out. A few days later he received a letter saying that before the package was opened all the copies were disposed of; please send 250 more. Major Cox did not have 250 copies to send but sent what he had. A few days later he received a letter from Detroit saying that there were several Negroes acting as book agents in Detroit selling "White America" to white people in Detroit. Within two weeks 17,000 copies of Major Cox's pamphlet were used in Detroit. Think of what that means! It means that the Negro in the United States is today awake; he is aroused; he listens no longer to the flattery and the blandishments of the politician; he is beginning to look facts in the face. It means that at least in Detroit, and I believe over the whole length and breadth of this land, the Negro is beginning to show more clearly the way towards a real solution of this problem than the white man who considered himself so wise.

It was a joy to me to realize that there were such men as the members of your organization in St. Louis and Detroit. It was a bitter mortification to me to realize that the members of your organization were doing spontaneously what I have been laboring for ten years to get the people of my race to do. And I want to congratulate you from the bottom of my heart for the courage and independence that you are showing in facing those facts and seeing them clearly and distinctly. And I speak to you not merely as a white American; I speak to you as a Virginian; I speak to you as the descendant of slave owners.

THE SOUTH DOES NOT HATE THE NEGRO

I want to say to you tonight that there is no decent white man in the South who can hate the Negro race; no decent man, no sane man who can have aught in his heart but feelings of kindliness and of gratitude towards the Negro race. As you have heard before, your people did not come here willingly; they were captured by force and violence; they were thrust in between decks in the horrible pest ships; they were brought to America, and when they thought they were going to breathe the free air of God's blue heaven and see God's green earth they found themselves still shackled in the chains of slavery. And why? There were forests to be cut down; there was land to be tilled; there was work of all kinds to be done, and the white man wanted the work done but did not want to take the trouble to do it himself. Your ancestors did that work; it is owing to their muscle, to their brawn, to their industry, to their good-will that this country made the progress in a few years that otherwise would have taken hundreds of years.

Not only that; but there never was a people who under hardship and oppression showed the spirit of kindliness and forgiveness which your people have shown. At a time when the armies of the South were fighting in a great war between the States—a war which was being fought on the part of the North to free you and your ancestors; at that very time, your people in the South stayed on the plantations, protected the women and children, raised the crops and sent the food to the front to the army that was fighting to keep them in slavery. And white people in the South know that; and white people in the South know what it means, and they are not insensible to feelings of gratitude and of thankfulness. We know what we owe you; we know it, and we intend that the whole world shall see that we appreciate this debt and pay it not only justly but generously. (Applause) . . .

Now, there is no use being sentimental; there is no use being visionary; we live in a practical time and we are practical people, and we have got to face facts; and the fact of the matter is that there is not a Negro in the United States of America today who is free; not one. The war did not make you free, and constitutional amendments did not make you free and the N. A. A. C. P. has not made you free. Why aren't you free? Let us go right down to the rock bottom of it. Why aren't you free? You have got magnificent people here in this country— people of learning, people of intelligence, people of culture, people of courage; yes. We are the first people to proclaim it to the world. Why is it that you are not free? What I am going to say to you is nothing new to you.

You are not free because the civilization that you are living under is not your own. (Applause.) That man would indeed be bold, who would deny to the Negro the possibility of the development of a higher order of civilization. Perhaps the Chinese may do it. Your civilization goes back 6,000 years. That white man (whose ancestors were going either naked or clad in skins through the jungles three thousand years ago) would be indeed bold who would assert that it was impossible for the Negro to develop his own civilization and his own culture. But it is perfectly sure that you will never do that in America. In America you have the position of intellectual and cultural parasites. No race can develop, no race can evolve unless it is standing on its own feet, and is supported by its own backbone. . . .

And I want to say to you that in my opinion and belief, if the white people in the South of this country realize that Marcus Garvey was standing not only for the salvation of his own race but for the salvation of the white race as well—if they realize that he had been railroaded into prison merely because he did not have a white face—if they realized what he stood for and what he meant, I believe that the South would rise to a man and demand that your great leader be released and restored to you. (Great applause.) There are some of us down there who realize that, and we are going to leave no stone unturned to spread that. Your enemies in your own race have the help and support of white people; white people give them money; white people go and flatter them and hold out false hopes to them and hobnob with them, and offer them social equality and put up money to help them; and some of those white people are people of great wealth and influence. I want to tell you this: that man for man we can match them; we will raise up for you and for your organization, man for man, as many as your opponents have among the whites of this country and they won't be whites who stay around in one district of the country; they will be whites from the North, from New England, from the Middle States; from the Southern Atlantic States, from the Gulf States, from the Middle West, from the Pacific Coast, from the far Northwest. It is coming and you will see it.

I noticed when I came in, the first things that struck my eye were some tags which all of you are wearing, and I looked at them and I saw "Let him go." I want to offer an amendment—free him; we don't want to let him go; we want to keep him here to do this work. (Thunderous applause.) And, my friends, if there is any honor in the American nation, I can promise you that when Marcus Garvey is free he shall not be deported.

17

Robert W. Bagnall:
The Madness of Marcus Garvey[1]

The collapse of the Black Star Line early in 1922, and Garvey's indictment on charges of mail fraud, led to some significant defections from the U.N.I.A. and encouraged his critics to step up their attacks. The opposition included much of the Negro press, a good part of the black clergy, and rival Negro organizations. One of these was the National Association for the Advancement of Colored People, whose chief spokesman, W. E. B. DuBois, as we have seen, had been one of the first to raise questions publicly about the Garvey movement. Garvey's critics were increasingly concerned about the delay in bringing his case to trial, and in January 1923 a "Committee of Eight" prominent American Negroes sent an open letter to Attorney General Harry M. Daugherty, asking that he "use his full influence completely to disband and extirpate this vicious movement, and that he vigorously and speedily push the government's case against Marcus Garvey for using the mails to defraud." One of the signers was Robert W. Bagnall, an N.A.A.C.P. official, who summarized his view of Garvey in a particularly bitter attack two months later in a Negro Socialist monthly magazine.

History tells the stories of a number of notable madmen who played quite a part for evil in their day. Nero, Caligula, Alexander are notorious instances. Literature furnishes us with a number of cases of madmen who thought themselves destined to do great things. The most striking of such characters is Don Quixote. This mad Knight tilted at wind-mills and thought them to be dragons and confused flocks of sheep with damsels in distress. The world has laughed at Don Quixote, but this old mad Knight was comparatively harmless. As mad as

[1] From Robert W. Bagnall, "The Madness of Marcus Garvey," *Messenger* 5 (March, 1923): 638, 648. Reprinted by permission of A. Philip Randolph. The quotation in the headnote is from the document printed in Amy Jacques Garvey, ed., *Philosophy and Opinions of Marcus Garvey*, vol. II (New York: Universal Publishing House, 1926), p. 299.

Don Quixote, the much advertised Negro demagogue Marcus Garvey appears to be, but is by no means harmless.

The following is a pen picture of this notorious character which those who know him say is an accurate likeness:

A Jamaican Negro of unmixed stock, squat, stocky, fat and sleek, with protruding jaws, and heavy jowls, small bright pig-like eyes and rather bull-dog-like face. Boastful, egotistic, tyrannical, intolerant, cunning, shifty, smooth and suave, avaricious; as adroit as a fencer in changing front, as adept as a cuttle-fish in beclouding an issue he cannot meet, prolix to the 'nth degree in devising new schemes to gain the money of poor ignorant Negroes; gifted at self-advertisement, without shame in self-laudation, promising ever, but never fulfilling, without regard for veracity, a lover of pomp and tawdry finery and garish display, a bully with his own folk but servile in the presence of the Klan, a sheer opportunist and a demagogic charlatan.

Until recent years many laymen supposed that a madman was violently irrational at all times and in all things. We now know that an insane man may be seemingly perfectly sane in many ways and at many times; his insanity being revealed only when certain choices, decisions and acts are presented to him. Often his insanity is confined to his reactions to certain departments of life. Our asylums are filled with individuals who can talk lucidly, intelligetly, and sanely on many questions, but who will reveal their condition to you by suddenly, calmly and assuredly announcing that they are Napoleon, or Cæsar, or a mighty king, general or magnate.

When Garvey was found guilty at a recent trial, Judge Panken of New York excoriated him, ending with these words—"There is a form of paranoia which manifests itself in believing oneself to be a great man." In this he infers that Garvey is afflicted with this form of insanity.

IS GARVEY A PARANOIAC?

We may seriously ask—, is not Marcus Garvey a paranoiac?

He certainly manifests many of the characteristic symptoms of this form of insanity. It is hard to understand many of the man's actions except on the assumption that he is insane—that he is a paranoiac. Let us examine the symptoms of paranoia and see how Garvey manifests them.

A paranoiac is afflicted with *Egomania*. His world is interpreted in terms of self. The first person of the personal pronoun is ever on his lips. One hears from him a succession of *I, Me*. The world revolves around *him*.

Read the *Negro World*. See how its pages are thick with the words

"I, Marcus Garvey" in every issue. See the self-laudation and egoism manifested there. Listen to Marcus Garvey as he speaks. Then you will think that the description I gave above of a paranoiac is one of Garvey. No sane man would be so gross in self-laudation as Garvey.

A paranoiac has delusions of grandeur. He thinks himself great.

FALSE IMAGINATION

The paranoiac will imagine himself a great leader or ruler or wonderfully gifted in some art; a genius. He thinks of himself always in the superlative. All others dwindle in comparison. He imagines that he has done great things. He craves acknowledgment of this from others. He has lost all sense of perspective. He can never receive enough fawning and flattery. Marcus Garvey when a soap boxer years ago in New York advertised himself as "the world's greatest orator." This title he still proclaims. He compares himself boastingly with Du Bois, James Weldon Johnson and others—claiming far greater attainments with nothing to substantiate his claims. He makes a mockery of the solid accomplishments of these gentlemen. He regards himself as an empire-builder, a divinely inspired leader of 400,000,000 Negroes (although no such number exists in the world).

He imagines miserable failures to be great successes and a credit to him. He confesses the loss of nearly a million dollars of poor people's money and that there is nothing left but debts. He confesses the utter loss of every vessel of his "Black Star Line," and then boasts of the success of his shipping line. In one breath he says that all three of his ships are gone; that there is nothing left out of nearly $1,000,000 but debts. In another breath he states that "if it hadn't been for our enemies, we would now have twenty vessels instead of three." He still seems under the delusion that he has three. He has a court reception, divides Africa in which he or his movement hasn't one foot of ground into duchies and makes "knights" and "ladies" and "dukes." Those presented to him must bend the knee before him. Arrayed in royal garb, he and his court assemble on an elevated dais while the common people are below, kept away from him by armed guards. Here is clearly a case of delusions of grandeur. Could a symptom be more characteristic?

The third symptom of a paranoiac is delusions as to fact. He suffers from exaggerated, distorted, perverted views of things. A paranoiac imagines an emaciated figure to be hale and sturdy and vice versa. He sees three people as a great crowd. Observe this trait in Garvey.

Marcus Garvey testified in court that the Yarmouth made three trips in three years, losing on one of these from two hundred and fifty thousand to three hundred thousand dollars ($250,000 to $300,000) and on another trip $75,000. Luc Dorsinville, the Haitian agent of the line, states that on another voyage the Yarmouth took three months to go from New York to Cuba, Haiti and Jamaica. The trip, he states, cost between $20,000 and $30,000 without enough cargo to pay half of that. Passengers booked were left waiting and $30,000 worth of cargo awaiting shipment was left on the dock in Haiti.

In spite of all this, Garvey in the *Negro World* of July 26, 1920, giving a report, states no losses whatever on his shipping lines.

In the *Negro World* of March 5, 1921, he says: "Nothing engineered by Negroes within the last 500 years has been as big or as stupendous as the Black Star Line. Today we control three-quarters of a million dollars (not on mere paper but in property value) and money that can be realized in twenty-four hours if the stockholders desire that their money be refunded to them. We can sell out the property of the Black Star Line and realize every nickel."

Less than eight months afterwards it was revealed that the line had nothing, that everything was gone.

He states that his organization has 4,500,000 members and is all over the world. An analysis of his financial report of 1921 reveals that he has not 20,000 dues paying members, and that his paying membership is much smaller than the National Association for the Advancement of Colored People.

He stated that 150,000 delegates would attend his convention. No more than 200 delegates were present as revealed by a careful analysis of the vote, day by day as given in the *Negro World*, his organ. Is it not clear that fact and fancy are sadly mixed and twisted in Garvey's mind?

UNDULY SUSPICIOUS

A paranoiac is unduly suspicious. He suffers from the delusion of persecution. He is always looking for treachery. He imagines someone is always trying to harm him.

Garvey's speeches are shot through with statements showing that the above is his frame of mind. He is continually talking of conspiracies and plots. His delusion is that he is the victim of persecution. Listen to these utterances of his and see if they are not the characteristic utterances of a paranoiac.

In the *Negro World* of January 21, 1921—"All the troubles we have had on our ships have been caused because men were paid to make this trouble by certain organizations calling themselves Negro Advancement Associations. They paid men to dismantle our machinery and otherwise damage it so as to bring about the downfall of the movement."

In the *Negro World* of May 13, he describes what is clearly a delusion of a great conspiracy. He says: "Millions of dollars were expended in the shipping industries to boycott and put out of existence the Black Star Line." He further says, "Bolshevists are paying for attacks on the line." (We wonder, in his insane delusions, how he gets capitalists and Bolshevists all against him.)

He continually changes his cabinet group. He finds traitors all about him. Everybody, he imagines, is his enemy. He brooks no criticism. He tolerates no adverse opinion.

"CASTLES IN SPAIN"

Another symptom of paranoia is that the victim imagines that when he desires a thing to be, it has come to pass. "Castles in Spain" to him are stone and mortar castles here. There is no clear differentiation between the ideal and the actual.

So Garvey sees himself president of the Republic of Africa, sees his government established. Year before last, at his convention, he promised that ninety days afterwards, he would have embassies at the court of St. James, in Paris, Petrograd, Rome, etc.

He has no conception of the gulf of difficulties between a plan and its fulfillment.

And in paranoia these delusions are fixed. No circumstances, logic or arguments can change them. So it is with Marcus Garvey.

There is much reason to believe that if Marcus Garvey were examined by alienists, he would be pronounced insane—a paranoiac.

If he is not insane, he is a demogogic charlatan, but the probability is that the man is insane. Certainly the movement is insane, whether Garvey is or not.

18
George Alexander McGuire: "Garvey's Work Shall Endure Throughout the Ages"[1]

As might be expected, the bitter attacks upon Garvey, and the collapse of most of his business enterprises, caused some decline in support for his movement in America and abroad. Many Garveyites remained steadfastly loyal, however, and viewed Garvey's imprisonment in 1925 as convincing proof of his assertion that Negroes could not expect justice in a white-dominated society, but must instead seek to establish a black country and government in the African motherland. One such loyal supporter was George Alexander McGuire, a former Episcopal priest who with Garvey had created the African Orthodox Church in 1921 as the spiritual arm of the Garvey movement. As archbishop and primate of the new church, McGuire urged Negroes to forget their white gods and to use black religious symbols, such as a black madonna and Christ, in their worship. Shortly after Garvey's imprisonment, McGuire contributed a preface for a volume of Garvey's collected speeches and writings in which he strongly defended his martyred leader and declared his faith in the ultimate triumph of Garvey's ideas.

Less than a decade ago Marcus Garvey appeared in Harlem—that crowded section of New York city which has been termed the "Mecca" of the Negroes of the world. Coming unheralded, like John the Baptist, he brought a message which carried conviction to all open-minded listeners. For many years previous Garvey had studied the hard lot of his race everywhere on God's earth. He had witnessed their political and economic oppression and noted the sufferings and discriminations which they experienced. He had himself drunk to the dregs of this bitter cup. As to Moses of old, so to Garvey, there came a clear call to

[1] From George Alexander McGuire, "Preface," in Amy Jacques Garvey, ed., *Philosophy and Opinions of Marcus Garvey*, vol. II (New York: Universal Publishing House, 1926), pp. v–viii. Reprinted by permission of Amy Jacques Garvey.

duty and leadership. As a member of a race free from the spirit of retaliation and vindictiveness, with the desire to treat all mankind as brothers without regard to differences in creed, race or country, this young man, while respecting the rights and admiring the progress of alien people, resolved to make the material, political, social and spiritual development of his blood-kin wherever found, and the fostering within them of the spirit of self-reliance, and self-determination, the sole consecrated purpose of his life, to the end that the Negro might eventually take his God-given place in the fraternity of man. Whatever successes Garvey has achieved, whatever efforts have failed of fruition, all were conceived and undertaken in the sincere and honest determination to attain for his race this great goal.

Not long ago Bishop Bratton, the white Episcopal Bishop of Mississippi, wrote a book dealing with the Negro under the title "WANTED LEADERS." The following is a statement of this friendly author: "The Negro has had, and still has, the tremendous task laid upon him of making the place which is his in life, and of taking it, not because he demanded it, but because he has successfully made that place. In general, he who has to DEMAND his place has never earned it. In general, too, he who has MADE a place has deserved it, and in the long run, it will be accorded him."

This is Garvey's philosophy in a nutshell as the unbiased and discriminating reader will discern in this collection of addresses and documents, by which the man must be judged rather than by the opinions of his adversaries or the miscarriage of any of his subsidiary undertakings. Garvey knew full well that the Negro had to make his place. Other leaders had either demanded or begged, but this new leader, the very type which the race wanted according to Bishop Bratton, came preaching to the Negro the necessity of making a place for himself which the world would be compelled to recognize and therefore to accord him.

Advocating and promoting racial organization, racial solidarity and racial self-government, he stimulated in Negroes both in this country and abroad, the spirit of nationalism and the desire for a republic of their own in their ancestral homeland. Millions enlisted under the banner of Marcus Garvey shouting the slogan "Africa for the Africans."

His phenomenal success, as well as his philosophy expressed in his vivid speeches which were broadcast throughout civilization, challenged the attention of those alien nations which dominate Africa and the antagonism of jealous and hostile Negro leaders in the United States of America. Demetrius of Ephesus, when he saw his occupation as a maker of gods threatened by the preaching of St. Paul against idolatry, called a convention of his fellow silversmiths to conspire against the great Apostle whose success would result not only in the cessation of the worship of the goddess Diana but the annihilation of the craft which had brought them wealth. These evil fellows led a mob through the streets of the city, and threw Ephesus into such confusion that the municipal authorities were compelled to take action, resulting in the departure of St. Paul to other parts. The professional Negro leaders of America have duplicated in many ways the strategy of Demetrius. No invective was too violent to express their censure, sarcasm and abuse; no shaft of contempt, ridicule or vilification too sharp to hurl at Garvey; no name in the lexicon too bad to be applied to him. He was called fool, fanatic, freak, deceiver, agitator and described as black, ugly, and an emissary of the Ku Klux Klan. "Garvey must go" was their war cry, and after pursuing various subterranean devices they succeeded in bringing about his imprisonment and are still hoping for his subsequent deportation from America.

Whether Garvey be in prison or out of prison, whether Garvey be living or dead, his vision of a free Africa, in which Negroes shall enjoy nationhood in governments of their own, shall one day become a reality. The Almighty Ruler of men and nations has predestined and spoken it, and Marcus Garvey is but the herald of a free and restored Africa. Newspaper reporters of both races treated Garvey's philosophy and preachments with levity, magnifying and exaggerating his commercial reverses. They intentionally or unintentionally hailed him as the Moses of a wholesale "Back to Africa" pilgrimage, a scheme which Mr. Garvey has never advocated nor planned. It is to be noted, however, that many publicists of the white race are approaching the viewpoint of Garvey and suggesting to America that she give aid and fostering oversight to the attainment of the aims of the Negroes within her borders, who desire to enjoy liberty in a government of their own in Africa.

Marcus Garvey's place in Negro history is secure for all time, despite his misfortunes which have been brought about both by opposition from without and treachery from within the camp. This man has felt the pulse of his people, and inspired them with race consciousness and hope in their future destiny more than any other leader, past or present. The great movement of which he has been the creator will "go on forever" like Tennyson's Brook until it reaches its consummation, for it is, in reality, a spiritual movement. Whether Garvey be in the flesh or in the spirit, the soul of the movement which he has fanned into flame, and the spiritual yearnings of his legions of converts will not be extinguished. Shed of its present physical habiliments the soul will be reincarnated and "go marching on."

To his followers Marcus Garvey is more than a leader. To them he is the outstanding prophet as well as the trail-blazer of the universal freedom of a noble race. Outsiders fail to understand the psychology of the disciples of Garvey, but the writer of this Preface (who is not ashamed to acknowledge that he is an open follower of this great teacher, rather than one of the numerous Nicodemuses who are secret disciples for fear of criticism or opposition) finds the reason for our devotion in the conviction that no man has spoken to us like this man, inculcating pride and nobility of race and pointing out to a down-trodden and discouraged people their Star of Destiny. This writer deems it an honor to prepare the foreword for this volume and seizes the opportunity to plead before the bar of an enlightened and fair-minded public opinion for Marcus Garvey, a man greatly misunder-stood in his plans for reformation. For, let it be known and acknowl-edged, Garvey is no idle dreamer, no empty visionary, no frenzied enthusiast, but rather a true reformer to whom it has been permitted to arouse his people from a condition of apathy growing out of hope-lessness and through good report or ill to suffer persecution, yea martyrdom for his race and the cause of truth, justice and liberty.

It is not Garvey who is being weighed in by the balance of the world's judgment, but his race, and particularly his jealous and un-worthy rivals who conspired against him. The Greeks gave Socrates, the greatest of their philosophers, the cup of hemlock. The Bohemians burned John Huss, their pioneer reformer, at the stake. Luther, Sa-vonarola and others suffered imprisonment and hardships for the truth's sake, but they were God's noblemen. So with Marcus Garvey, a man of intellectual power and penetrating vision; a man who dis-covered the only solution of the problem confronting the Negro people the world over; and had the courage to preach the new gospel of salva-tion from permanent economic and political servitude. Disgruntled leaders who delight in the fleshpots of Egypt or accept gratefully, the crumbs which fall from the political master's table, while secretly protesting against the injustices of the color-line, concentrated their attack upon Garvey for proclaiming this a white man's country with a white man's government in which the black man's place is strictly limited and clearly defined, and beyond which it has been declared he "shall not pass."

While in theory they have vehemently denied this doctrine of Gar-vey, they have been compelled to accept it in practice, vainly hoping for the political and social millennium in America, when they shall hold the highest offices of State and enjoy the fullest privileges of society. But because Garvey believes with all his soul, and preaches with all his fervid eloquence the doctrine of racial integrity to be secured and maintained in a Negro country and government free from the pollution of miscegenation, his rivals who claim that at all hazards they must fight on American soil for their social, political and economic rights, have heaped opprobrium upon him.

Marcus Garvey in prison, with a conscience untainted from the guilt of fraud to deceive and prey upon his own people for personal gain, poor in pocket, although he has handled millions of dollars, eagerly and willingly contributed by his followers, suffers gladly with determined soul and unbroken spirit. No trace of cowardice has been found in him, even by his bitterest foes, for it is his courage to proclaim his convictions and to attempt the realization of his vision which has removed him from the sphere of his activities. Consecration of a great cause still leads to Calvary, but Calvary is not the scene of the final act of a people's redemption or of a reformer's victory. "Via Crucis" is still the path to permanent achievement, glory and honor. Garvey's work shall endure throughout the ages. His dreams of "Africa for the Africans" shall surely be fulfilled.

19
Should the Garvey Movement Be Saved or Destroyed?[1]

Garvey's critics usually expressed grudging admiration for his organizational skills but disagreed over the value of his movement—and particularly over whether it could or should be salvaged for what they considered more productive purposes following his conviction and imprisonment. The stocky Jamaican had undeniably succeeded as had no previous Negro leader in reaching and inspiring the black masses, and there was much speculation about the future of Garveyism. Some Negro Communists, fascinated by Garvey's creation of the first mass movement of lower-class blacks, argued that the Universal Negro Improvement Association should not be permitted to decline but should be redirected into civil rights and anti-imperialist activities on behalf of black workers in America and elsewhere. Other erstwhile opponents argued that Garvey's emphasis on black racism and African redemption offered little of promise for American Negroes and that the movement should accordingly be destroyed. The following articles represent both sides of the debate within the black community about the future of Garveyism.

SALVAGE THE U.N.I.A.: A COMMUNIST VIEW

The Universal Negro Improvement Association, the largest of all Negro organizations, is in danger of going to pieces. A split is impending, if a split has not already occurred.

The Universal Negro Improvement Association

A breaking up of this Negro association would be a calamity to the Negro people and to the working class as a whole. We say this not because the program or the leadership of the organization is of good quality, but because the Universal Negro Improvement Association is

[1] From Robert Minor, "Death or a Program!" *Workers Monthly* 5 (April, 1926): 270, 271, 272–73, 281; reprinted by permission of *Political Affairs*. "The U.N.I.A.," *Messenger* 5 (1923): 782; reprinted by permission of A. Philip Randolph.

bigger than its leadership, and the deficiencies of its program are directly due to deficiencies of its leaders. The organization itself represents the first and largest experience of the Negro masses in self-organization. It is the largest organization that ever existed among the Negroes of the United States and the West Indies. It claims a large membership in Africa and it certainly has some followers among seafaring Negro workers in many parts of the world. It is composed very largely, if not almost entirely, of Negro workers and impoverished farmers, altho there is a sprinkling of small business men. In any case the proletarian elements constitute the vast majority of the organization. Within its ranks are gathered the largest number of those energetic figures among working class Negroes who have arisen to activity in the period since the world war. We believe that the destruction of such an organization of the Negro masses, under the circumstances, would be a calamity.

And the destruction seems to be an imminent danger. It also appears on the surface to be the threatened result of a selfish quarrel among ambitious leaders. . . .

However, it is an entirely false appearance from which one would judge that the present crisis is due solely to a quarrel among individuals. Anyone who has watched the affairs of this organization during the past several years ought to know that there are deep social causes for the threatened disruption. The Universal Negro Improvement Association has been the victim of a leadership which turned it away from the struggles that were demanded of it. Therefore the organization, as expressed in its leadership, has during the past five years been steadily undermining its own reason for existence.

At the first substantial convention of the organization held in New York in 1920, it was apparent that the period of mass organization among Negroes of the working class (not merely organization of intellectuals) which had been made possible by the social changes of and following the world war, was beginning, and that it was crystallizing more largely in the U. N. I. A. than elsewhere. Also the rather primitive and unclear expression of working class character in the movement was exhibited by the program adopted in 1920. . . .

But it is certain that fatal weaknesses were present in the organization, and that Garvey, altho he was undoubtedly the chief builder of the organization, was also the chief one that carried into it the poison of opportunism. Upon any movement of a mass character which seeks to organize a large section of the exploited classes, there always begins to be exercised a tremendous pressure. The whole super-structure of capitalist society invariably rushes to its task of adjusting any mass movement in such a manner as to eradicate any tendencies incompatible with the capitalist social system. The effects of such pressure soon began to be apparent in the U. N. I. A., and especially in the trend of Garvey himself. Many incidents, especially occurring in the attempts to organize Negroes in the southern cities, brought out sharply the fact that the organization would be fought most bitterly on those issues which had to do with the demands of the Negro masses for organization in trade unions, for political rights, and especially those demands which struck out in the direction of the abolition of the general system of social inequality.

Under the pressure, Garvey began to give way. Difficulties were encountered by the organizers of the U. N. I. A. on the ground that the organization had "bolshevistic" qualities leading toward economic, political and social equality. Garvey met every difficulty by disclaiming the portions of his organization's program which were under attack at the given moment. By a process of elimination, all demands which were offensive to the ruling class were dropped one by one, and the organization settled down to a policy of disclaiming any idea whatever of demanding any rights for the Negro people in the United States— the policy of declaring that the Universal Negro Improvement Association was not striving to attain any political or social rights of the Negro in America, but was trying only to construct an organization which would bring about the establishment of a "home for the Negro people in Africa." From a negative protestation, the policy evolved into a positive declaration (voiced by Garvey and acquiesced in by his followers) that the Universal Negro Improvement Association recognized the United States as a "white man's country," and that it was therefore opposed to social equality in this country for the Negro. . . .

All of the old program adopted in 1920 has disappeared from sight. Today if you ask for the program of the U. N. I. A., you are told, in the words of Garvey that "our one purpose, our one object, is the planting of the colors of the Red, the Black and the Green as the African standard that shall give to us a country, a nation of our own."

Garvey had, according to his own statements, confined every hope and aim to this one thing. Inevitably this resulted in 1921 in narrowing the chief operation down to the sale of stock in a steamship company, the Black Star, reorganized after prosecution, under the new name of Black Cross Line, which was expected to open up resources with the help of American and other Negroes.

Anything that might destroy the illusion of a peaceful penetration into Africa would of course be a severe blow to the structure that Garvey had built.

Garveyite Illusions Blasted

Along came events which destroyed the illusion.

Apparently Garvey did not operate this stock selling plan in a manner free from charlatanry, and the excuse that he had sold stock under false pretenses became the one under which he was finally sent to prison by the United States government, after a shamefully arbitrary trial with all the qualities of a political frame-up.

But that was not all that served to destroy the illusion. The after war unrest of the suppressed peoples of Africa—the early prelude to the present Morocco trouble, the Egyptian independence movement, etc., had given their alarm to the British, French, Belgian and Spanish governments, and these began taking measures to exclude Garvey's organization and its publications from African colonies. This tended to confine operations to the "independent" republic of Liberia as distinguished from the outright possessions of imperialist powers. The Universal Negro Improvement Association concentrated on Liberia, and according to Garvey's claim, the Liberian government gave a large concession to the Universal Negro Improvement Association (or a subsidiary) for the development of Liberia's rubber and other resources. Upon the claim of the concession to develop the natural resources of Liberia, Garvey based his sole remaining hope.

But the illusion was still further to be exploded. The American ruling class does not let anything of value in the way of rubber lands lie around loose. A series of quick and very mysterious operations between Calvin Coolidge, Harvey Firestone, Solomon Porter Hood (a Negro tool of the Firestone Rubber Company appointed by Coolidge as American Minister to Liberia) took place in the summer of 1924 simultaneously with the final arrest and conviction of Garvey and his imprisonment in the federal penitentiary at Atlanta. Garvey went to prison at the same moment that the concessions he claimed in Liberia were given to the Firestone corporation. It may be that a shrewd prosecutor can show a perfect legal case against Garvey (perhaps a case equally as strong as the case against Mr. Mellon's Aluminum Company), but we know that "perfect cases" are only incidental to the political purposes of prosecutions by the American capitalist government. Garvey was sent to prison because the American government thought that his imprisonment would be an effective blow at the Negro masses, to break up their organization (any Negro mass organization is considered dangerous per se, regardless of Utopian programs), and also perhaps because the imprisonment of Garvey incidentally relieved the Firestone deal of a petty annoyance.

But what has been the effect upon the internal affairs of the Universal Negro Improvement Association?

The effect has been to destroy the possibility of any further illusion of the magic acquisition of the continent of Africa by the "business" operations of an association of Negroes, while the war in Morocco, and the rapidly sharpening struggle against imperialism thruout Africa, helped to wash away the picture of benevolent British statesmen and American millionaires making a present of a continent larger than North America, ladened with untold gold, diamonds, rubber, and every imaginable wealth, to a group of helpless, down-trodden and exploited Negroes, out of pure love and Christian kindness.

The one center of the Garvey program had become incredible even to Garvey's credulous followers.

The single foundation stone upon which Garvey had built was thus destroyed. The Universal Negro Improvement Association could not be held together any longer on the basis of any belief in the Zionistic program. The Universal Negro Improvement Association, kicked off of the basis of the Liberia illusion but still clinging to the exploded Zionism of Garvey, awakened by the imprisonment of Garvey whose powerful personality was a cohesive force, has inevitably drifted to the point of disruption.

The final refusal to release Garvey, under the circumstances, finally precipitated the crisis. It is known that Garvey will be deported (unless an effective protest is made) at the close of his prison term. The result is that thruout the organization the scramble to succeed him in control has come.

Garvey Adopts the Ku Klux Klan "Race Purity" Theory

But while the controversy was boiling with all the appearance of being a mere quarrel of individual leaders without any fundamental issues involved, an incident occurred at Richmond, Va., which shows the true nature of the crisis the organization faces. It appears that the Richmond organization of the Universal Negro Improvement Association, having a membership of between 200 and 300, was called together for the purpose of hearing a lecture by three of the most reactionary, Negro-hating, propagandists of "white supremacy." These were John Powell, Major Ernest Cox and Major Percy Hawse. It appears that one or more of these three men is involved in the effort to pass thru the Virginia state legislature a so-called "race integrity" law, forbidding intermarriage of Negroes with white people. The Ku Klux Klan bases its Negro-baiting theories upon an idiotic concept of "race purity." Garvey has adopted this by attempting to make a supreme virtue of "race purity" for the Negro. This imaginary "race purity" (there is no such thing as an unmixed race) is supposed to be a basis upon which the Negro hater and the Negro can reach a common understanding, and on this theory the Negro masses are expected to sit and listen in a receptive mood to the propaganda of those who wish to make the Negro perpetually submit to race discrimination in the matter of segregation, discrimination, separate schools, and anti-intermarriage laws. But it appears that the membership of the Negro organization was not quite so idiotic as the Garvey leadership had assumed. A number of Negro workers arose in the meeting and objected vigorously to allowing the enemy propagandists to speak. The membership supported the objectors, and the three Negro baiters were driven out of the hall by the protest. The Richmond division faces a split, with the left wing clamoring for a repudiation of Garvey's concession that "this is a white man's country."

The Revolt of the Left Wing

We believe that this incident points to the real basis of the crisis of the Universal Negro Improvement Association. The new Negro—a healthy working class left wing in the organization—refuses any longer to submit to the servile anti-Negro program that Garvey has been adopting to thrust down their throats. . . .

Upon the rank and file of sincere Negro workers in the organization, and upon these more active spirits, the ultimate hope of saving and revitalizing the Universal Negro Improvement Association depends.

The key to the matter is the question of a program of militant struggle for the rights of the Negro here in the United States, in addition to an effective anti-imperialist world program.

It is a case of a program or death, for the Universal Negro Improvement Association.

DESTROY THE U.N.I.A.: A SOCIALIST VIEW

Much has been said anent the future of the U. N. I. A. since the incarceration of its leader, Marcus Garvey. The question seems to be: Should it be saved or destroyed? We hold that the U. N. I. A. represents Garveyism or the spirit of segregation, of the Ku Klux Klan, that the United States is a white man's country and that hence Negroes should migrate where there are no white people, wherever that is. If Garvey is a menace, his spirit is a menace, hence the U. N. I. A. should be destroyed. It demoralizes the spirit of the Negroes' fight for economic, political and social betterment, for it accepts the dictum of Chief Justice Tainey [sic], viz.: "that a Negro has no rights which a white man is bound to respect."

20
E. Franklin Frazier:
Garvey as a Mass Leader[1]

Whether or not they approved of his objectives, Garvey's contemporaries were invariably impressed by his charismatic leadership qualities and by his success in building a mass movement of international scope in a comparatively brief time. Black intellectuals did not join the Garvey movement in large numbers, and many of them emphatically rejected Garveyism, but even his critics generally demonstrated some ambivalence bordering on grudging admiration when they considered Garvey's organizational achievements. This ambivalence was apparent in an early scholarly assessment of the Garvey movement offered in 1926 by a young black sociologist, E. Franklin Frazier, who over the course of his subsequent career became one of the foremost students of the American Negro.

The Garvey movement is a crowd movement essentially different from any other social phenomenon among Negroes. For the most part American Negroes have sought self-magnification in fraternal orders and the church. But these organizations have failed to give that support to the Negro's ego-consciousness which the white masses find in membership in a political community, or on a smaller scale in Kiwanis clubs and the Ku Klux Klan. In a certain sense Garvey's followers form the black Klan of America.

The reason for Garvey's success in welding the Negroes into a crowd movement becomes apparent when we compare his methods and aims with those of other leaders. Take, for example, the leadership of Booker Washington. Washington could not be considered a leader of the masses of Negroes, for his program commended itself chiefly to white people and those Negroes who prided themselves on their opportunism. There was nothing popularly heroic or inspiring in his program to captivate the imagination of the average Negro. In fact the Negro was

[1] From E. Franklin Frazier, "Garvey: a Mass Leader," *Nation* 123 (August 18, 1926): 147–48. Reprinted by permission of the Nation Associates, Inc.

admonished to play an inglorious role. Certain other outstanding efforts among Negroes have failed to attract the masses because they have lacked the characteristics which have distinguished the Garvey movement. It is only necessary to mention such an organization as the National Urban League and its leadership to realize that so reasoned a program of social adjustment is lacking in everything that appeals to the crowd. The leadership of Dr. DuBois has been too intellectual to satisfy the mob. Even his glorification of the Negro has been in terms which escape the black masses. The Pan-African Congress which he has promoted, while supporting to some extent the boasted aims of Garvey, has failed to stir any considerable number of American Negroes. The National Association for the Advancement of Colored People, which has fought uncompromisingly for equality for the Negro, has never secured, except locally and occasionally, the support of the masses. It has lacked the dramatic element.

The status of Negroes in American life makes it easy for a crowd movement to be initiated among them. In America the Negro is repressed and an outcast. Some people are inclined to feel that this repression is only felt by cultured Negroes. As a matter of fact many of them can find satisfaction in the intellectual and spiritual things of life and do not need the support to their personalities that the average man requires. The average Negro, like other mediocre people, must be fed upon empty and silly fictions in order that life may be bearable. In the South the most insignificant white man is made of supreme worth simply by the fact of his color, not to mention the added support he receives from the Kiwanis or the Klan.

Garvey came to America at a time when all groups were asserting themselves. Many American Negroes have belittled his influence on the ground that he is a West Indian. It has been said that Garvey was only able to attract the support of his fellow-countrymen. The truth is that Garvey aroused the Negroes of Georgia as much as those of New York, except where the black preacher discouraged anything that threatened his income, or where white domination smothered every earthly hope. Moreover, this prejudice against the West Indian Negro loses sight of the contribution of the West Indian to the American Negro. The West Indian who has been ruled by a small minority instead of being oppressed by the majority, is more worldly in his outlook. He has been successful in business. He does not need the lodge, with its promise of an imposing funeral, or the church, with its hope of a heavenly abode as an escape from a sense of inferiority. By his example he has given the American Negro an earthly goal.

Garvey went even further. He not only promised the despised Negro a paradise on earth, but he made the Negro an important person in his immediate environment. He invented honors and social distinctions and converted every social invention to his use in his effort to make his followers feel important. While everyone was not a "Knight" or "Sir" all his followers were "Fellow-men of the Negro Race." Even more concrete distinctions were open to all. The women were organized into Black Cross Nurses, and the men became uniformed members of the vanguard of the Great African Army. A uniformed member of a Negro lodge paled in significance beside a soldier of the Army of Africa. A Negro might be a porter during the day, taking his orders from white men but he was an officer in the black army when it assembled at night in Liberty Hall. Many a Negro went about his work singing in his heart that he was a member of the great army marching to "heights of achievements." And even in basing his program upon fantastic claims of empire, Garvey always impressed his followers that his promise was more realistic than that of those who were constantly arguing for the theoretical rights of the Negro. In the *Negro World* for October 18, 1924, he warned his followers that

> Those who try to ridicule the idea that America is a white man's country are going to find themselves sadly disappointed one of these days, homeless, shelterless, and unprovided for. Some of us do harp on our constitutional rights, which sounds reasonable in the righteous interpretation thereof, but we are forgetting that righteousness is alien to the world and that sin and materialism now triumph, and for material glory and honor and selfishness man will slay his brother. And in the knowledge of this, is the Negro still so foolish as to believe that the majority of other races are going to be so unfair and unjust to themselves as to yield to weaker peoples that which they themselves desire?

And after all this is essentially what most Negroes believe in spite of the celebrated faith of the Negro in America.

A closer examination of the ideals and symbols which Garvey always held up before his followers shows his mastery of the technique of creating and holding crowds. The Negro group becomes idealized. Therefore he declares he is as strongly against race-intermixture as a Ku Kluxer. He believes in a "pure black race just as all self-respecting whites believe in a pure white race." According to Garvey, civilization is about to fall and the Negro is called upon "to evolve a national ideal, based upon freedom, human liberty, and true democracy." The "redemption of Africa" is the regaining of a lost paradise. It is always almost at hand.

This belief has served the same purpose as does the myth of the general strike in the syndicalist movement. Garvey, who is dealing with people imbued with religious feeling, endows the redemption of Africa with the mystery of the regeneration of mankind. He said on one occasion: "No one knows when the hour of Africa's redemption cometh.

It is in the wind. It is coming one day like a storm. It will be here. When that day comes, all Africa will stand together."

Garvey gave the crowd that followed him victims to vent their hatred upon, just as the evangelist turns the hatred of his followers upon the Devil. Every rabble must find someone to blame for its woes. The Negro who is poor, ignorant, and weak naturally wants to place the blame on anything except his own incapacity. Therefore Garvey was always attributing the misfortunes of the Negro group to traitors and enemies. Although the identity of these "traitors" and "enemies" was often obscure, as a rule they turned out to be Negro intellectuals. The cause for such animosity against this class of Negroes is apparent when we remember that Garvey himself lacks formal education.

Garvey who was well acquainted with the tremendous influence of religion in the life of the Negro, proved himself matchless in assimilating his own program to the religious experience of the Negro. Christmas, with its association of the lowly birth of Jesus, became symbolic of the Negro's birth among the nations of the world. Easter became the symbol of the resurrection of an oppressed and crucified race. Such naive symbolism easily kindled enthusiasm among his followers. At other times Garvey made his own situation appear similar to that of Jesus. Just as the Jews incited the Roman authorities against Jesus, other Negro leaders were making the United States authorities persecute him.

Most discussions of the Garvey movement have been concerned with the feasibility of his schemes and the legal aspects of the charge which brought him finally to the Atlanta Federal Prison. It is idle to attempt to apply to the schemes that attract crowds the test of reasonableness. Even experience fails to teach a crowd anything, for the crowd satisfies its vanity and longing in the beliefs it holds. Nor is it surprising to find Garvey's followers regarding his imprisonment at present as martyrdom for the cause he represents, although the technical charge on which he was convicted is only indirectly related to his program. But Garvey has not failed to exploit his imprisonment. He knows that the average man is impressed if anyone suffers. Upon his arrest he gave out the following statement: "There has never been a movement where the Leader has not suffered for the Cause, and not received the ingratitude of the people. I, like the rest, am prepared for the consequence." As he entered the prison in Atlanta he sent a message to his followers which appeared in his paper, the *Negro World*, for February 14, 1925. He paints himself as a sufferer for his group and blames his lot on a group of plotters. In commending his wife to the care of his followers he says: "All I have, I have given to you. I have sacrificed my home and my loving wife for you. I intrust her to your charge, to protect and defend in my absence. She is the bravest little woman I know." Such pathos he knew the mob could not resist, and the final word he sent to his supporters under the caption, "If I Die in Atlanta," with its apocalyptic message, raises him above mortals. He bade them "Look for me in the whirlwind or the storm, look for me all around you, for, with God's grace, I shall come and bring with me the countless millions of black slaves who have died in America and the West Indies and the millions in Africa to aid you in the fight for liberty, freedom, and life."

Since his imprisonment Garvey has continued to send his weekly message on the front of his paper to his followers warning them against their enemies and exhorting them to remain faithful to him in his suffering. It is uncritical to regard Garvey as a common swindler who has sought simply to enrich himself, when the evidence seems to place him among those so-called cranks who refuse to deal realistically with life. He has the distinction of initiating the first real mass movement among American Negroes.

PART THREE

GARVEY IN HISTORY

Early assessments of the Garvey movement, especially those by Negro intellectuals, tended for the most part to be critical, stressing Garvey's shortcomings and failures, and lamenting that so little of enduring value had resulted from his promising mass movement. Indeed, for more than a generation after Garvey's exile from the United States, his work and ideas received scant and generally negative treatment in books dealing with the recent history of American Negroes. In discussing the twenties some black writers ignored Garvey entirely, perhaps because they disagreed fundamentally with his black separatist ideas and were embarrassed or dismayed by the extent of his popular following. Others portrayed him as a strutting buffoon, a roguish charlatan, a power-hungry egomaniac, who had cleverly exploited the frustrations and the meager savings of his unsophisticated followers. Gradually in the years after Garvey's death, however, a more balanced and generally much more positive view emerged, particularly after most of Africa, as well as Jamaica and other predominantly black Caribbean islands, achieved independence from white colonial rule, and as younger black militants in the United States and elsewhere rediscovered Garvey's black nationalist philosophy and sought to recreate another black power mass movement.

21

James Weldon Johnson: Glitter Instead of Substance[1]

The early critical view of Garvey is typified by James Weldon Johnson, whose close ties to the integrationist National Association for the Advancement of Colored People, which had

[1] From James Weldon Johnson, *Black Manhattan* (New York: Alfred A. Knopf, 1930), pp. 256–59. Reprinted by permission of the Estate of James Weldon Johnson.

*led the fight against Garvey, naturally influenced his thinking
about the U.N.I.A. leader. Johnson's treatment of Garvey in his
widely read* Black Manhattan, *published in 1930, helped to establish the dominant view of the Garvey movement for the next
generation.*

Within ten years after reaching New York Marcus Garvey had
risen and fallen, been made a prisoner in the Atlanta Federal Penitentiary, and finally been deported to his native island. Within that
brief period a black West Indian, here in the United States, in the
twentieth century, had actually played an imperial role such as Eugene
O'Neill never imagined in his *Emperor Jones.*

Garvey failed; yet he might have succeeded with more than moderate success. He had energy and daring and the Napoleonic personality, the personality that draws masses of followers. He stirred
the imagination of the Negro masses as no Negro ever had. He raised
more money in a few years than any other Negro organization had
ever dreamed of. He had great power and great possibilities within
his grasp. But his deficiencies as a leader outweighed his abilities. He
is a supreme egotist, his egotism amounting to megalomania; and so
the men surrounding him had to be for the most part cringing syco-
phants; and among them there were also cunning knaves. Upon them
he now lays the entire blame for failure, taking no part of it to himself. As he grew in power, he fought every other Negro rights organization in the country, especially the National Association for the
Advancement of Colored People, centering his attacks upon Dr. Du
Bois.

Garvey made several vital blunders, which, with any intelligent
advice, he might have avoided. He proceeded upon the assumption of
a triple race scheme in the United States; whereas the facts are that
the whites in the United States, unlike the whites of the West Indies,
make no distinction between people of colour and blacks, nor do the
Negroes. There may be places where a very flexible social line exists,
but Negroes in the United States of every complexion have always maintained a solid front on the rights of the race. This policy of Garvey,
going to the logical limit of calling upon his followers to conceive of
God as black, did arouse a latent pride of the Negro in his blackness,
but it wrought an overbalancing damage by the effort to drive a wedge
between the blacks and the mixed bloods, an effort that might have
brought on disaster had it been more successful.

He made the mistake of ignoring or looking with disdain upon the
technique of the American Negro in dealing with his problems of

race, a technique acquired through three hundred years of such experience as the West Indian has not had and never can have. If he had availed himself of the counsel and advice of an able and honest American Negro, he would have avoided many of the barbed wires against which he ran and many of the pits into which he fell.

But the main reason for Garvey's failure with thoughtful American Negroes was his African scheme. It was recognized at once by them to be impracticable and fantastic. Indeed, it is difficult to give the man credit for either honesty or sanity in these imperialistic designs, unless, as there are some reasons to suppose, his designs involved the purpose of going into Liberia as an agent of development and then by gradual steps or a coup taking over the government and making the country the centre of the activities and efforts for an Africa Redeemed. But thoughtful coloured Americans knew that, under existing political conditions in Africa, even that plan could ultimately meet with nothing but failure. Had there been every prospect of success, however, the scheme would not have appealed to them. It was simply a restatement of the Colonization Society scheme advanced just one hundred years before, which had occasioned the assembling of the first national convention of Negroes in America, called to oppose "the operations and misrepresentations of the American Colonization Society in these United States." The central idea of Garvey's scheme was absolute abdication and the recognition as facts of the assertions that this is a white man's country, a country in which the Negro has no place, no right, no chance, no future. To that idea the overwhelming majority of thoughtful American Negroes will not subscribe. And behind this attitude is the common-sense realization that as the world is at present, the United States, with all of its limitations, offers the millions of Negroes within its borders greater opportunities than any other land.

Garvey's last great mistake came about through his transcending egotism. He had as leading counsel for his trial Henry Lincoln Johnson, one of the shrewdest and ablest Negro lawyers in the country. But the temptation to strut and pose before a crowded court and on the front pages of the New York newspapers was too great for Garvey to resist; so he brushed his lawyers aside and handled his own case. He himself examined and cross-examined the witnesses; he himself harangued the judge and jury; and he was convicted.

Garvey, practically exiled on an island in the Caribbean, becomes a somewhat tragic figure. There arises a slight analogy between him and that former and greater dreamer in empires, exiled on another island. But the heart of the tragedy is that to this man came an opportunity such as comes to few men, and he clutched greedily at the glitter and let the substance slip from his fingers.

22
Robert Hughes Brisbane, Jr.: Building Black Self-Esteem[1]

For more than a decade after Garvey's death in 1940, he was largely forgotten except by a tiny remnant of faithful U.N.I.A. members who kept in touch with their leader's widow in her Jamaican homeland. In the 1950s, however, there came a gradual reawakening of interest in the Garvey movement, as scholars, most of them too young to have personal knowledge of or to be affected by the bitter feuds of the 1920s, began to study the historical significance of Garveyism. One of the first of these scholarly reappraisals was offered by a young professor at Morehouse College, Robert Hughes Brisbane, Jr., who stressed Garvey's role in rebuilding Negro race pride.

For a people in whom the lore of the Old Testament was so deeply ingrained, Garvey quite easily filled the role of a Messiah. The race had long likened its condition to that of the Hebrews held in Egyptian bondage. Pan-Africanism promised redemption and freedom which seemed forever denied in America. Thus Garvey could consistently evoke frenzied applause with such statements as the following:

We are striking homeward toward Africa to make her the big black republic. And in the making of Africa the big black republic what is the barrier; the barrier is the white man, and we may say to the white man who dominates Africa that it is to his interest to clear out now because we are coming, not as in the time of Father Abraham 200,000 strong but we are coming 400,000,000 strong and we mean to retake every square inch of the 12,000,000 square miles of African territory belonging to us by right divine.

[1] From Robert Hughes Brisbane, Jr., "Some New Light on the Garvey Movement," *Journal of Negro History* 36 (January, 1951): 58–60, 60–62. Copyright © 1951 by The Association for the Study of Negro Life and History, Inc. Reprinted by permission of the publisher and the author.

The lack of genuine self-esteem and race pride was a problem for which Garvey also had a solution. He insisted that the Negro's inferiority complex was due, primarily, to his acceptance of alien standards of beauty, that the race was foolishly overlooking its own gifts, grace and beauty in a frustrating emulation of the whites. Hence, there was to be no more intra-racial derision and caricaturing of the thick-lipped, kinky-haired black. These were nature's badges for the African; let him be proud of them. To fill the apparent void of the Negro's past, Garvey resurrected and refurbished ancient African civilizations. For the first time in their lives, many American Negroes heard of the glories of Nubia and Ethiopia and learned that Ancient Egypt had had at least a Negroid population. Indeed, in Garvey's words, "when the great white race of today had no civilization of its own, when white men lived in caves and were counted as savage, this race of ours boasted a wonderful civilization on the banks of the Nile."

In the early 1920's, Garvey occupied a disputed but firmly established place of leadership among the world's Negro population. Even his severest critics admitted that his followers were numbered in the millions. Every Garvey venture was supported enthusiastically. His newspaper, the *Negro World*, established in 1917, quickly became the world's leading Negro publication; the ships of his ill-fated Black Star Line carried millions of dollars in Negro investments to the ocean bottom with them and it was the money of his worshipers which equipped his abortive promised-land colony in Liberia. For American Negroes, however, the really important thing about Garveyism was not its promised-land feature. While most American Negroes would have been proud of the existence of a powerful Negro nation in Africa, few of them actually contemplated migrating to the Dark Continent to aid in its erection. Basically, Garveyism was a new creed, one which accelerated the re-education of the Negro, helped reconstruct his values and to re-orientate his outlook on his past and future. Under the stimulus of Garveyism, Negro nationalism became creative, constructive, boastful, and definitely more chauvinistic.

What has become known as the Negro Renaissance reached its full flowering during the high tide of the Garvey movement. In the field of literature, young Negro writers and poets turned to the Dark Continent for the subjects of new verses. . . .

The serious study of the Negro's past begun in 1915 by Carter G. Woodson won several brilliant young recruits during the Garvey era. Such men as J. A. Rogers and Arthur Schomburg rummaged through libraries and collections the world over in search of material dealing with the Negro's history. The new outlook was manifested also in the realms of music and art. The importation of African art, barely a trickle before World War I, swelled to a virtual torrent during the early twenties. African sculptures in clay, wood, ebony, and ivory became prized and eagerly sought for. Negro composers on the other hand devoted a new interest to African themes and rhythms.

To summarize and tie up the new trends, *Opportunity*, a Negro periodical edited by Charles S. Johnson, produced in May, 1924 an African Art issue containing African-inspired poems by Claude McKay, Langston Hughes and Lewis Alexander. The publication ran other African Art numbers in 1926 and 1928.

The new pride in things black and things African fathered a drive on the part of the Negro press to substitute the term black men for colored men and Afro-American for American Negro. Gradually, Negroes learned to refer to their African ancestry and heavy pigmentation less self-consciously.

In the realm of politics, Garveyism accelerated the shift of the Negro electorate from the Republican to the Democratic Party. Among other things, the new Negro considered himself a radical. He was beginning to distrust the hide-bound traditionalism of Republican political leaders and specifically the Negro element in this group. The new self-confidence and spirit of independence among the black masses in the Northern and Eastern metropolises was manifested in new allegiances between the black electorate and Democratic political machines. On the economic front the teachings of Garvey ran parallel to those of Booker T. Washington. Both men were interested in the establishment of a sound and thriving Negro bourgeoisie. Garvey particularly hammered away at the necessity for the building of Negro factories, the organizing of cooperative markets among American Negroes, and the establishment of international trade among the world's black population. During his heyday numerous attempts were made by his followers to establish Negro enterprises. In general, however, Garvey's economic doctrine produced little of lasting benefit to the race. For, existing off race loyalty in the main, black business enterprises could not maintain the wage levels or working conditions of their white competitors. On the other hand, the Negro consumer like everyone else bought where prices were cheapest. He should not have been expected to invest in race loyalty when it meant less for his dollar. In passing, perhaps it should be mentioned that the followers of Garvey were among the leaders of the abortive Jobs For Negroes Campaigns which blossomed in Northern cities during the early 1930's.

To the clique of Negro leaders whom Garvey easily overshadowed during his sojourn in America, this West Indian figure was embarrassing, dishonest and disruptive of the gradual progress they considered the race to be making under their guidance. For Garvey they reserved their most violent, vituperative and scurrilous attacks. One of these men, Robert W. Bagnall, described Garvey as being "fat and sleek with protruding jowls; small bright piglike eyes and rather full doglike face." It was because of the initiative of these men that Garvey's career in America finally ended with a prison term and deportation.

In the long run, however, the meteoric flash of Garvey's rise awed even his bitterest enemies and some of the more thoughtful among them eventually paid him the high tribute of emulation. For one fleeting moment Garvey managed to turn the attention of America's black internal proletariat homeward to Africa. His most solid accomplishment, however, was to help gird this group with the confidence and self-esteem needed in the long hard struggle for its historical objective of full integration—the bridging of the gap between the *in* and *of* of American society.

23

Ben F. Rogers:
DuBois and Garvey[1]

*Any consideration of Garvey's place in history must in-
evitably also involve that of W. E. B. DuBois—one of Garvey's
chief rivals for leadership of the Negro world in the 1920s—whose
sharp editorial criticism in the NAACP organ,* Crisis, *had sparked
the "Garvey Must Go" campaign. In comparing DuBois and
Garvey, the historian Ben F. Rogers concluded that both had
serious weaknesses, but that a combination of their better qualities might have led to real and lasting achievements.*

To face realistically the problems of race riots, lynchings, and
the growing power of the Klan, the Negroes needed leaders. For a
generation, in time of crisis they had turned to Booker T. Washington,
but Washington had died in 1915. There were, however, two Negroes
of marked ability who, during the early 1920's might have been successful in providing the much needed leadership.

The first of these was William Edward Burghardt DuBois, a hand-
some bronze mulatto, of Negro, French, Dutch, and Indian ancestry.
Born in Massachusetts shortly after the Civil War, DuBois had been
educated at Fisk, Harvard, and Berlin. His doctoral dissertation on
The Suppression of the African Slave Trade had been published as
number one of the *Harvard Historical Studies* and is still the standard
work on the subject. But DuBois was more than a historian. In Phila-
delphia and later while teaching at Atlanta University, he had pio-
neered in the sociological study of the Negro. DuBois had also spoken
out against Booker T. Washington's conciliatory policies as early as
1903, and had been the acknowledged leader of a small militant anti-
Washington group of Negro intellectuals during the first years of the
twentieth century. When the National Association for the Advancement of Colored People had been founded in 1909, DuBois had left

[1]From Ben F. Rogers, "William E. B. DuBois, Marcus Garvey, and Pan-Africa,"
Journal of Negro History 40 (April, 1955): 155–56, 158–59, 162–65. Copyright ©
1955 by The Association for the Study of African-American Life and History, Inc.
Reprinted by permission of the author and publisher.

his job at Atlanta University to go to work for the Association, and since 1910, he had been the editor of its journal, the *Crisis*. In this position he had fought long and hard for civil rights and against segregation. His leadership, however, was wholly in the field of ideas. Haughty and restrained, he did not have the magnetism necessary to attract a large personal following. As he himself admitted, "I never was, nor ever will be, personally popular." Nevertheless, DuBois had many of the qualities of leadership. His intellect was great, his understanding broad, his pen facile, and his reputation well-established.

At this juncture, however, DuBois chose to subordinate the realities of the American situation to a great ideal in which he had long been interested—the Pan-African movement. "The problems of the American Negro," he wrote, "must be thought of and settled only with continual reference to the problems of the West Indian Negroes, the problems of the French Negroes and the English Negroes, and above all of the African Negroes." For the next ten years, DuBois was to devote a great deal of his time and energy to the calling of a series of Pan-African Congresses which would, he hoped, eventually bring the Negroes of the world together into a great international pressure group. . . .

Certainly, DuBois' preoccupation with his esoteric Pan-African Congresses was in part responsible for the fact that the Negro masses, desiring a solution to their problems, turned in great numbers during the early 1920's to Marcus Garvey. Garvey, a West Indian Negro of moderate education and attainments, had entered the United States in 1916. Like DuBois, Garvey had for many years considered the possibility of uniting all the Negroes in the world into one great organization, and he had made an abortive attempt in 1914 to set up a Universal Negro Improvement Association in Jamaica. New York City, however, seemed to have possibilities far beyond those of the West Indies, and so in 1917 Garvey reorganized the U.N.I.A. and in the following year began publishing the *Negro World*, a weekly paper disseminating his Pan-African ideas. Negroes immediately began to flock to his banner, and there is little question that Marcus Garvey was the most popular Negro leader in the United States during the early 1920's.

What was it that gave him this immense influence? Why was his Pan-Africanism any more attractive than that of DuBois? In part, of course, it was his dynamic personality, his great oratorical powers, and his shrewd understanding of psychology. But Garvey's success was due not only to his native abilities; it was due also to the appeal of the ideas he set forth.

The cornerstone of Garvey's teaching was pride in race. He urged Negroes to be proud of their black skins and their great heritage. He preached the superiority of black over white. He satisfied himself and his followers that the angels were black and that Satan and his imps were white. He founded his own African Orthodox Church, whose bishop preached vigorously against the idea of a white God, and in 1924, the *Negro World* advertised an approaching meeting where the race would "spiritually Deify the Black Man of Sorrows and Cannonize (sic) the Black Virgin Mother." Admission 50c. Garvey's appeals to race pride even extended to the point of urging Negro clubs to white-ball undesirable applicants for membership and of proposing to erect in Washington a Black House where a duly elected Negro would act as leader of his race for a four year term.

The reason that the average Negro had a feeling of inferiority, according to Garvey, was that in the United States his race was in the minority. The motto of his Association was "No Law but Strength: No Justice but Power," and clearly the white race had the power. Negroes could expect oppression. Race riots and lynchings were not abnormal; they were to be expected. In North America, said Garvey, the Negro was living "on the fringe of the civilization of others," and if he remained there, in the end he would be "completely obliterated."

The only salvation then for American Negroes was to join Garvey's organization and prepare to return to Africa where they could establish a government of their own strong enough to protect colored people everywhere. The machinery needed to create this so-called African Republic was set up in Harlem in 1921. Garvey became the Provisional President of Africa and surrounded himself with a newly created African nobility. There was also the African Legion, Garvey's private army, resplendent in dark blue uniforms with red stripes. There were Black Star Nurses and bands and choirs. All the paraphernalia of the New Africa was ready for action whenever the master spoke. . . .

Though Garvey was an excellent fund raiser, he was far less expert as manager of a shipping company. When the Black Star Line failed, the Federal government investigated Garvey's activities and charged him with using the mails to defraud thousands of trusting Negroes. Brought to trial, Garvey, in his immense ego, discharged his attorney and undertook his own defense, but he could not persuade the jury of his innocence. Found guilty, he received the maximum sentence, a one thousand dollar fine and five years in jail.

There is no question that the Black Star Line was a fiasco, but the severity of the judgment against Garvey is perhaps an indication that the government was using the mail fraud case in an effort to destroy his powerful influence. Why though should the government of the United States be particularly interested in doing away with Garvey? Perhaps the answer to this question may be found in the fact that the Garvey movement was based not only on personal attraction and appealing ideas; it was also based in a most insidious way on force. Negroes who criticized him were threatened and often viciously attacked. Street fights became numerous between his friends and enemies. Those who complained because they lost money in the Black Star Line were told to be quiet or else. At meetings, the officers of the African Legion came prepared for trouble with riding crops or swords and made sure none got in without the proper tickets of admission. One particularly vigorous anti-Garvey editor received through the mails a human left hand and a warning to stop his talk. After Garvey's indictment, the chief government witness was murdered by two officials of the U.N.I.A. Several participants in the trial complained of attempts at intimidation, and one of Garvey's lieutenants was found guilty of contempt for threatening two witnesses. There was some evidence then at the height of the movement that Garvey was attempting, as one of his critics claimed, to create a Black Ku Klux Klan.

Garvey's conviction pleased DuBois who was convinced that now the Negroes were rid of "the worst phase of Garveyism." From 1924 on, DuBois seemed to assume that the Garvey movement had ceased to exist, an assumption followed by many later writers, and an assumption which has no basis in fact.

Having been found guilty, Garvey took upon himself the role of martyr. Thousands of his followers packed Liberty Hall week after week, and in March 1924, almost a year after the conclusion of his trial, the New York *Times* reported a Garvey meeting of 6,000 in Madison Square Garden in the afternoon and one of 10,000 at night. While he was in prison, floods of telegrams urging his release continually descended on Washington, and when he was released in 1927 and deported through New Orleans, the New York *Times* reported a crowd of 500 Negroes standing in the rain to cheer him.

Even more amazing than this evidence of Garvey's continuing popularity, however, is the fact that he was able to get his followers to invest in another steamship line. While he was at large, after having been convicted in the mail fraud case, he incorporated the Black Cross Navigation and Trading Company and sold enough stock to buy another ship. The christening was attended by United States Congressman Royal A. Weller, and three thousand Garveyites braved a downpour and paid 50c a head to look at the ship. Anticlimatically enough, the Black Cross Trading and Navigation Company followed the Black Star Line into bankruptcy.

It was also after Garvey's trial and conviction that he made his first real attempt to establish a colony of American Negroes in Africa. Later critics have scoffed at the impracticality of any migration, but it is interesting to note that in 1924, the Liberian government was so worried for fear the U.N.I.A. would take over their country that they warned all of their American consuls to deny visas to any of Garvey's followers. Two ex-presidents of the country were members of the Association, and the mayor of Monrovia held the title of High Potentate of Africa in Garvey's Provisional Government. This initial attempt at migration failed not so much because of the American Negro's apathy as because of the Liberian government's opposition, which Garvey called "treachery of the lowest order."

The egotistical Garvey, sold on his own ideas, had nothing but contempt for DuBois' "shadowy Pan-African Congress." In 1923, the *Negro World* reported that DuBois' London meeting "was attended by less than a dozen persons." DuBois, the article continued "had no more right or authority to have called a Pan-African Congress than a cat had to call together a parliament of rats."

If Garvey was critical of the Congresses, he was super-critical of DuBois. To him, DuBois was the personification of all the forces seeking to destroy his movement. Whenever Negro editors or the N.A.A.C.P. attacked Garvey, he saw DuBois behind it all. DuBois was his scapegoat, and for a decade, the *Negro World* poured out vitriolic abuse upon him. According to Garvey he was a "conceited pedant," a "liar," a "lazy dependent mulatto," and an "envious narrow-minded man." He despised the poor, was content with being a secondary part of white civilization, and wore a pointed beard like a Frenchman's. The failure of the Black Star Line, the Black Cross Navigation and Trading Company, and the Liberian venture could all be laid to the obstructionist tactics of DuBois. He was read out of the race at the U.N.I.A.'s fourth annual convention, and he was the subject of a pamphlet authored by Garvey, "W. E. Burghardt DuBois as a Hater of Dark People." Wholesale 10c; retail 15c. Surely these bitter attacks did not strengthen DuBois' position as a Negro leader.

Thus the efforts of the American Negroes to find adequate leadership in the early 1920's were largely frustrated. DuBois had the necessary intellect and ability, but he had little appeal for the Negro masses. Garvey, with his dynamic and attractive personality, was at best a poor organizer and at worst a downright charlatan. A combination of the better qualities of the two might have led to real accomplishment.

24
Theodore G. Bilbo:
A Divine Afflatus[1]

*Garveyism's stress upon racial purity and separatism,
as well as the possibility of a large scale repatriation of American
Negroes to Africa, continued to attract the support of Southern
white racists long after the movement itself had declined. Only a
year before Garvey's death he received high praise from Senator
Theodore G. Bilbo of Mississippi, a racist politician whom many
American blacks regarded as an implacable enemy. The occasion
was Bilbo's sponsorship of a bill supported by a number of Negro nationalist groups, including the American branch of the
U.N.I.A., which proposed that the war debts owed the United
States by European nations be used to provide funds for the
repatriation of several million American Negroes to Liberia.
Despite Garvey's editorial support from London (see Chapter
10), nothing came of the Bilbo scheme.*

The most gratifying thing in my life is to be able today to
present to the American Congress petitions signed by two and one-half
million American Negroes pleading and begging for a physical separation of the races. By their act in signing these petitions to be resettled
in their fatherland—Africa—they say to the world, "We are proud of
our race; we believe in racial integrity; we are not willing to have our
blood stream commingled with the white blood. We want to flee from
this certain disaster that is going to overtake both races by complete
amalgamation and the production of a mongrel race."

These petitioners know that in saving their race they are likewise
saving ours. They have faith in their ability to work out their own
destiny and establish a nation in a country all their own, where they
can reach their highest destiny in a land of freedom—a land without
oppression and a land without discrimination.

I call the attention of the Senate to the presence of these petitions.

[1] From *Congressional Record*, April 24, 1939, pp. 4650–51, 4652, 4665–66.

135

The signatures have been carefully counted, and the petitions have been signed by two and a half million Negroes of the United States. I may add that the petitions come from every State in the Union, praying and asking for a physical separation of the races, or that an opportunity be afforded the Negroes to be resettled in their fatherland.

The Vice President: The petitions presented by the Senator from Mississippi will be received and referred to the Committee on Foreign Relations.

Mr. Bilbo: Mr. President, there is ample evidence that the Negro nationalists, who support this bill, have chosen between the alternative solutions of race problems—between separation and amalgamation—for they have given a wide circulation to the privately published race studies of Earnest Sevier Cox, of Richmond, Va. The works of this author deal with the nature of race problems, rather than with the various phases of the problem, and there has been a close and long friendship between this author and the Negro leaders of the nationalistic movement.

At this point I wish to read into the RECORD, for the information of the Senate and of the country, the titles of these splendid publications by Colonel Cox. They are White America, Let My People Go, The South's Part in Mongrelizing the Nation, and Lincoln's Negro Policy.

In this connection, since the press of the country has given notice of the introduction of a bill on this subject by me, I wish to read some telegrams which I received this morning. First, I read a telegram from Cleveland, Ohio, as follows:

> CLEVELAND, OHIO, *April 24, 1939.*
> I am pleased that through your efforts the Senate will receive the resettlement program of the American Negro in his fatherland. We in Cleveland are 100 percent behind you. I feel that if the Negro will ever become a man he must be placed back in his fatherland.
> STIENBART DYER.

I received the following telegram from Tampa, Fla.:

> TAMPA, FLA., *April 24, 1939.*
> We congratulate you in sponsoring the program for American Negroes returning to their fatherland.
> DIVISION No. 272, U. N. I. A.,
> JOHN WIGGS, *Secretary.*

The following telegram came from Jacksonville:

JACKSONVILLE, FLA., *April 23, 1939.*

Senator THEO G. BILBO,
  United States Senate, Washington, D. C.:
  Your law abiding citizens, followers of the martyred African Princess Laura Adorkor Koffey, assassinated Miami, Fla., March 8, 1928, in hearty accord with your views as published under your name in Chicago Defender of April 22, 1939. Prayerful wishes for your continued interest and courageous efforts in this cause so thoroughly misrepresented by an element of our visionless misleaders.

MISSIONARY AFRICAN UNIVERSAL CHURCH, INC.

This telegram came from New York:

NEW YORK, N. Y., *April 24, 1939.*

Senator THEODORE BILBO,
  Senate Chamber:
  Ten thousand Negroes of the Universal Negro Improvement Association, assembled in mass meeting, endorse your proposed repatriation bill. Hoping for the full support of your fellow Senators.

GARVEY CLUB, INC.
G. E. HARRIS, *President.*
C. A. WRIGHT, *Secretary.*

•   •   •

[*Mr. Bilbo*]: In conformity to a pledge to that effect made to the Senate, and to the 2,000,000 or more citizens of the United States of African descent interested in migrating to Liberia, I now offer a bill to provide for the liquidation and settlement of the war debts due the United States; to create a bureau of colonization and to provide for the migration and colonization of United States citizens to newly acquired territory; to provide aid to United States citizens desirous to migrate to the Republic of Liberia, and for other purposes. The bill declares the intent of Congress to be that the benefits and provisions thereof shall apply to citizens of the United States who may qualify as eligible for citizenship in the Republic of Liberia, and who, by their physical fitness and climatic adaptability, may qualify as migrants to be permanently settled in the territory to be acquired, and who shall have voluntarily expressed a desire to become migrants under the provisions of the bill. . . .

Mr. Bilbo: Mr. President, let me say in this connection that the impression seems to prevail in the minds of some people, especially some of our colored friends, and especially among the newspaper element of our colored friends, that the proposal to provide for the resettlement of the American Negro in his fatherland is all a plan of my own. An attempt would naturally be made on the part of some of these amalgamationists, miscegenationists to prejudice the proposal because I am a Senator representing the South. I wish to say that I am pursuing and prosecuting the campaign for this great program which means the salvation of both the white and the black races, with the support of millions of Negroes, in every State in the American Union, as evidenced by the petition which is on my desk, representing two and one-half million American Negroes. . . .

Following the death of Bishop Henry McNeil Turner, Marcus Garvey, a Negro born in Jamaica, took up the movement of repatriation; and during the course of his activities he developed into the most powerful and effective advocate of race integrity and race nationality that this country or any other country has ever known. We are told by authorities who have devoted effective study to the labors of Garvey on behalf of the Negro race that he was a man of good education, and that in his youth he brooded long over the disadvantages suffered by his race. He organized a Universal Negro Improvement Association. He stressed the importance of blood integrity and race nationality. He spoke in a language that stirred the deep desire of the race for these essentials. Garvey's organization became international. It developed into a vast empire of workers devoted to the achievement of economic progress through racial integrity and race nationality. It is said that the membership of the organization at one time exceeded 6,000,000. Its membership came from many foreign countries, as well as from the States of the Union.

Garvey was the first repatriationist who succeeded in gaining to any appreciable degree the attention of the American press. As stated by Mr. Earnest Sevier Cox, this organization, in a plan to aid Liberia, believed that it had acquired certain rights in that country, and sent out a shipment of goods of the value, it is said, of $50,000, when the Liberian end of the agreement was rescinded.

At about this time other American citizens were successful in acquiring holdings in Liberia; but these other Americans, not being of Negro descent, could not become citizens of Liberia or hold title to its land. The Firestone Tire & Rubber Co. has $90,000,000 invested in a rubber plantation in Liberia on leased land. This obstacle was overcome by leasing a million acres of Liberian land for a period of 99 years. Garvey opposed the white man's occupation of Africa through the seizure of Liberian lands on long leases. He advocated the doctrine of "Africa for the Africans," and decried the white man seizing Negro Africa and holding its people in subjection there, as the white man had done elsewhere.

Garvey's enemies were legion. More especially he was stubbornly fought by the Negroes in the United States who favored amalgamation —the blending of the blood of the two races. Notwithstanding this formidable opposition, more forcefully felt through the activities of the N.A.A.C.P., Garvey succeeded in gaining a powerful hold upon the group of the Negro race which may be designated as "Afro-Americans," practically full-blooded Negroes.

Garvey made an effort to finance the Black Star Line of steamships to be used to carry Negro emigrants to Africa and to develop trade among Negro people. This unfortunate enterprise resulted in temporarily arresting his repatriation movement. He was convicted of having fraudulently used the mails to sell stock in the Black Star Line. His conviction took place just before the economic collapse known as the depression. The presiding judge denominated him as an impractical dreamer, afflicted with a Messianic complex, and considered that the innocent Negroes of the country should be protected against the vagaries and impractical schemes of the repatriation idealist.

It may be true that Garvey sold stock in the Black Star Line. It may be true that the Black Star Line went to pieces as an investment. However, there was no more reason for penalizing Garvey for selling that kind of stock than there was for penalizing bankers who flooded the country with Peruvian bonds and other bonds which were sold through the mails and which were just as worthless as the stock in Garvey's Black Star Line.

In passing, it may be well to note that shortly after Garvey's conviction multiplied millions of dollars' worth of stock issued by so-called practical men—men free from the hallucinations of a Messianic complex—proved to be as worthless as the stock in the Black Star Line. President Coolidge commuted Garvey's sentence; but since he was an alien he was automatically exiled from the United States. His imprisonment deprived him of further active leadership in the great organization he had founded. His largest group of followers was located in the United States; and because of his alienation he was powerless to carry on the great movement of repatriation.

When we consider that Garvey's work was terminated by a court conviction and subsequent deportation, we find cause for discouragement among his followers. However, the chief value of his labors lay in the quickening of a race consciousness and in the birth among his followers of a new hope for racial integrity and Negro nationality. For this service he could not be adjudged in violation of law by any court in the world, while on the other hand he was denominated a benefactor of the human race at the bar of enlightened public opinion.

The most significant thing about the achievement of Garvey is that notwithstanding the collapse of his colonization program at the zenith of its popularity, notwithstanding the loss of considerable sums of money invested by the members of his race, notwithstanding his conviction and imprisonment, followed by deportation from the country in which he had established his great organization—notwithstanding all these things and more, the movement he had originated did not die with the passing of its founder. The longing for economic freedom and progress, the yearning for the establishment of Negro nationality, the burning desire to make secure racial integrity that Garvey had implanted in the souls of millions of Afro-Americans, survived. He definitely succeeded in establishing the fact that there is an overmastering impulse, a divine afflatus among the mass of Negroes of the United States for a country of their own and a government administered by themselves. Garvey was the greatest of the Negro publicists, and the most conspicuous organizer of his race.

25

Robert G. Weisbord:
Garvey's Ultimate Victory[1]

Despite the central importance of the United States for his movement, Marcus Garvey remained a British citizen throughout his life, spending his last years in London, where he died in 1940. Yet the British government, with its extensive empire in Africa and the Caribbean, understandably found little of comfort in the activities of this black subject. The extent of Whitehall's concern can now be more accurately determined with the recent opening of the files of the Colonial Office and the Foreign Office for the period encompassing the heyday of the Garvey movement. As historian Robert G. Weisbord has noted, after reviewing these British records, Garvey would no doubt have been flattered had he known fully of the attention he commanded from British officials on three continents, just as he would surely be gratified at the acceptance today of so many of his ideas throughout the black world.

Future historians may well view Marcus Mosiah Garvey as the central figure in twentieth-century Negro history. Some students of America's seamy record of race relations, not to mention countless ghetto militants, already regard Garvey as the patron saint of black nationalism and the progenitor of Black Power. Curiously, though he reached the zenith of his fantastic career while residing in the United States, Garvey was born in Jamaica, remained a British subject during his entire lifetime, spent his declining years in Britain, and died in relative obscurity in London in 1940. More than any other black leader, the charismatic Garvey in his world-wide activities underlined the international character of the colour problem. He was a pan-Negroist without equal.

During his era Great Britain could still boast of an empire con-

[1] From Robert G. Weisbord, "Marcus Garvey, Pan-Negroist: the View from Whitehall," *Race* 11, no. 2 (April, 1970): 419, 427–28. Published for the Institute of Race Relations, London, by the Oxford University Press. © 1970 by the Institute of Race Relations. Reprinted by permission of the Institute of Race Relations.

taining a sizeable number of the four hundred million coloured people
for whom Garvey was the self-proclaimed leader. Therefore, Whitehall's concern with Garvey, especially in his heyday, is not at all surprising. The depth and scope of that concern have not been fully
understood. Fortunately, pertinent Foreign Office and Colonial Office
documents, until recently inaccessible to scholars, are now open for
examination at the Public Record Office in London. Dispatches from
embassies, legations, and consulates on at least three continents re-
peatedly touched on the threat posed by Garvey and his local followers
during the years of his American period (1916–27). . . .

Generally, it may be said that as apprehensive as the British were
about the destructive impact that Garvey might have on the Empire,
they felt that the United States Government was chiefly responsible
for him within its borders. U.N.I.A. activities in British colonies or
in countries where British interests were vitally involved were another
matter. Garvey's *Negro World* was banned in many dependencies; and
members of the U.N.I.A. were denied entry to others. Just days after
Garvey was convicted in June 1923 for using the mails to defraud investors in the Black Star Line, the Foreign Office began to predict his
moves after imprisonment. If, after the expiration of his term, Garvey
applied for a passport to travel to any British West African colonies,
facilities were not to be granted. Ironically, Garvey, the passionate
apostle of 'back-to-Africanism,' never did set foot on African soil.

Garvey would doubtlessly have been amused by the way in which
British officials impugned his motives. One minuted in 1923 that "it
is more than suspected that Garvey's efforts . . . are not without considerable financial profit to himself and his immediate associates." As
previously mentioned, the Governor of British Honduras saw Germany
as the evil force behind Garveyism. Others claimed that the U.N.I.A.
was linked with the "Wobblies," the International [*sic*] Workers of the
World. In the judgment of one observer, Garvey's paper attacked
Britain "with a malignity reminiscent of the *Irish World*." Clearly,
Negro World malignity was no greater than that of an official who
lamented in 1924 about Garvey: "It's a pity the cannibals do not get
hold of this man."

Die-hard champions of the erstwhile British Empire might well
share those intemperate sentiments for the reverberations of Garveyism are still being felt. *Mzee* Jomo Kenyatta, putative leader of the
Mau Mau and today President of an independent Kenya, once related
to C. L. R. James:

> how in 1921 Kenya nationalists, unable to read, would gather round a
> reader of Garvey's newspaper, the *Negro World,* and listen to an article
> two or three times. Then they would run various ways through the for-

est, carefully to repeat the whole, which they had memorised, to Africans hungry for some doctrine which lifted them from the servile consciousness in which Africans lived.

On the eve of independence Kwame Nkrumah acknowledged Ghana's debt to Marcus Garvey. And in his autobiography Nkrumah stated that Garvey's *Philosophy and Opinions* did more to fire his enthusiasm than any other book. James Coleman in his book *Nigeria: Background to Nationalism* has written that: "Many themes in latter-day Nigerian nationalism have been cast in the spirit if not in the exact words of Garvey." Garveyite ideas deeply impressed Nigerians who were involved in proto-nationalistic organizations such as the Nigerian Youth Movement and the National Congress of British West Africa.

Ten years after his death, the Kingston *Gleaner* stated:

> . . . it would be true to say of Jamaica, and to a lesser extent of the other British West Indies, that national consciousness received its main impetus, if it was not actually born, from the racial movement associated with the still revered Marcus Garvey.

Fittingly, a bust of Garvey now graces King George VI Memorial Park in Kingston and a thoroughfare is named in his honour. His remains were disinterred and taken to Jamaica in 1964.

Today in England itself Garvey is lauded, even deified, by Black Power advocates from the West Indies and Africa. In a very real sense, as far as the British Empire is concerned Garveyism has triumphed. Whitehall had had good reason to be worried.

26
George Shepperson:
Garvey as Pan-Africanist[1]

No doubt part of the basis for the opposition of W. E. B. DuBois to the Garvey movement was Garvey's program of African redemption, which made the U.N.I.A. the voice of black Africa in the New World and thus a serious rival to DuBois's own Pan African Congresses, the first of which was held in Paris in 1919. The bitter feud between Garvey and DuBois in the 1920s precluded any cooperation between them with respect to Africa, despite their obvious common interest in the Negro homeland. Both men nevertheless made significant contributions to pan-Africanism, though, as the British historian George Shepperson points out, it is important to recognize their distinctively different roles.

The term "pan-Africanism" has been bandied about in recent years with disturbing inaccuracy. A striking example of this occurs in the highly publicized Twentieth Century Fund's *Tropical Africa* (New York, 1960, II, p. 280) which in a most inadequate section on African nationalism says, "In Garveyism the alloy of pan-Africanism was smelted into the ore of Ethiopianism." It would be difficult to find more misunderstandings of the nomenclature and processes of African politics in so few words. If misleading assertions of this sort can appear in such an elaborate and expensive study in 1960, the time has surely arrived when historians should come to the aid of synoptic students of Africa, the "pan-Africanism" of whose academic approach has become so individual that it distorts out of all recognition the Pan-African movement and the pan-African movements.

It may be found helpful, both in tracing the origins of "pan-Africanism" and in employing the term accurately in studies of contemporary

[1] From George Shepperson, "Pan-Africanism and 'Pan-Africanism': Some Historical Notes," *Phylon* 23 (Winter, 1962): 346–48. Copyright © 1962 by Atlanta University. Reprinted by permission of the publisher.

African politics, to use, on some occasions, a capital "P" and, on others, a small one. If a collective term is required, "all-African" is useful.

"Pan-Africanism" with a capital letter is a clearly recognizable movement: the five Pan-African Congresses (1919, Paris; 1921, London; 1923, London and Lisbon; 1927, New York; 1945, Manchester), in all of which the American Negro scholar, Dr. W. E. B. DuBois, played a major part; it is linked with the publication of George Padmore's *Pan-Africanism or Communism?* (London, 1956) and with the first All-Africa People's Conference at Accra in December 1958. It is for this movement that Dr. Nkrumah claims Ghana has a special destiny.

On the other hand, "pan-Africanism" with a small letter is not a clearly recognizable movement, with a single nucleus such as the nonagenarian DuBois. (Students of the role of "chance" in history should find it interesting to speculate on what Pan-Africanism would have become without DuBois's longevity.) It is rather a group of movements, many very ephemeral. The cultural element often predominates. The complicated history of négritude is a good example of this. Briefly, pan-Africanism with a small letter may be used for all those all-African movements and trends which have no organic relationship with the capital "P" variety.

Faced with such a dichotomy—which is, clearly, not absolute and in which there are obvious interacting elements—one is justified in asking where Marcus Garvey and his Universal Negro Improvement Association (U.N.I.A.) fit into this schema. Early writers on Pan-Africanism often spoke of Garvey as if he were the leader of this movement. Ch. du Bus de Warnaffe, for example, writing of "Le mouvement pan-nègre aux Etats-Unis et ailleurs" in *Congo* (Brussels) for May, 1922, devoted almost the whole of his article to the Garvey movement. In the 1920's also, R. L. Buell spoke of Garvey as the leader of the Pan-African movement. At that time, such an approach was understandable. In 1920 the U.N.I.A. convention in New York issued its great "Declaration of Rights of the Negro Peoples of the World" and Garvey stood out as the leader of a mass movement, whereas the more remote and intellectual DuBois had a restricted following.

Yet the *leit-motiv* of American Negro political history at this time was the bitter personal feud between the two men. It is the very bitterness of this rivalry which makes it difficult to fit Garvey and his followers into the Pan-African movement with a capital letter, as defined above. His overt racialism would suggest that he belongs to cultural pan-Africanism. And, of course, as a movement the U.N.I.A. was in decline after 1927 when its leader was expelled from the United States. Furthermore, Garvey had none of DuBois's longevity, dying at the age of fifty-three in 1940.

If one adopts the classification suggested above, Garveyism should be excluded from Pan-Africanism with the capital letter in the days when DuBois was in direct control of this movement. When this ceased and leadership passed into African hands between 1945 and the founding of the State of Ghana, Garveyism comes into Pan-Africanism with a capital "P."

This Pan-African rehabilitation of Garvey probably dates from the Manchester Congress of 1945 at which, if DuBois was nominally in control, effective leadership was in the hands of a predominantly African group, of which Padmore and Nkrumah were joint political secretaries and Jomo Kenyatta was assistant secretary. An article by Garvey's second wife appeared in the May, 1947, issue of *Pan-Africa* which had sprung out of the Manchester Congress. After that, the road was open for a full-scale rehabilitation of Garvey by the heirs of DuBois. The measure of the change can be seen by referring to Padmore's assertion in 1931 that "The struggle against Garveyism represents one of the major tasks of Negro toilers in America and the African and West Indian colonies" and the statement in his 1956 book that "Despite his obvious limitations as a diplomatist and statesman, Marcus Garvey was undoubtedly one of the greatest Negroes since Emancipation, a visionary who inspired his race in its upward struggle from the degradation of centuries of slavery." Additional tribute was paid the following year when Kwame Nkrumah's autobiography was published in which he stated that the *Philosophy and Opinions of Marcus Garvey* influenced him more than anything else during his stay in the United States. And when the State of Ghana was established it superimposed on its new national flag a black star, recalling Garvey's Black Star Line, after which, eventually, the Ghanaian shipping company was to be called. The seal was set on this process of rehabilitating Garvey when a preparatory paper for the 1958 All-Africa People's Conference at Accra coupled him with DuBois as an outstanding contributor to the spread of the idea of Pan-Africanism and, as if noting that a major shift in ideology was taking place, asserted that "Though Garvey never used the word PAN-AFRICA, he planned and laboured to establish a PAN-AFRICAN nation."

In sum, it may be said that when the Pan-African movement was in predominantly American Negro hands, Garveyism was an embarrassment to it; but when Africans took over the leadership, it became almost an essential element. Of course, there are limitations to this rehabilitation. The Back-to-Africa movement which had been an integral part of Garveyism was allowed to lapse, although a close tie has been maintained in Ghana and elsewhere in West Africa with Negroes from the United States and the West Indies, particularly the professional elements, the "talented tenth" in DuBois's words. And, of course, any form of socialism was anathema to Garvey, whereas today it is an essential part of the Padmore-Nkrumah nucleus of Pan-Africanism.

The implications of this analysis of Garveyism are that before the late 1940's, when Garvey had been dead for nearly a decade and a respectable interval had elapsed for some of the scars of his old feud with DuBois to heal, it is best classified under pan-Africanism with a small letter and that after this it becomes part of Pan-Africanism.

27
Jabez Ayodele Langley:
Garvey and African Nationalism[1]

Although most students of the Garvey movement have credited it with stimulating the growth of black nationalist sentiment in Africa, it has always been difficult to measure very precisely the degree and extent of Garvey's influence there. One can easily note such negative signs of Garvey's presumed appeal as the banning of his newspaper, the Negro World, *by apprehensive colonial authorities, but it is harder to determine the varied reactions of native Africans, especially those of limited education, to the Garvey movement. Some Liberian officials, for example, embraced Garveyism with enthusiasm; the hostility of others led to the abrupt about-face of the Liberian government in 1924, when it expelled the Garveyite colonizers. One of the first scholars to attempt a detailed assessment of Garvey's influence on African nationalism was Jabez Ayodele Langley, of the Centre of African Studies at the University of Edinburgh.*

Nearly every work on African nationalism has asserted the influence of Garveyism on the growth of race consciousness in Africa. The nature of this influence is more often asserted than analysed. The testimonies of the King of Swaziland (who is reported to have told Mrs. Garvey that the only two black men he knew in the Western world were Jack Johnson, the boxing champion, and Marcus Garvey) and ex-President Nkrumah (who recollects that Garvey's *Philosophy and Opinions* had a profound influence on him during his student days in America) are usually cited as examples of Garvey's influence on African nationalist thought and politics. As Professor Essien-Udom has pointed out in his introduction to the second edition of Garvey's *Philosophy and Opinions,* "Garvey's influence on the Negro freedom movements

[1] From Jabez Ayodele Langley, "Garveyism and African Nationalism," *Race* 11 (October, 1969): 157–58, 159–60, 163–65, 169–70. Published for the Institute of Race Relations, London, by the Oxford University Press. © Institute of Race Relations, 1969. Reprinted by permission of the Institute of Race Relations.

in the United States and Africa, will never be fully known." Sufficient material now exists in African and American sources for a preliminary assessment of the extent and significance of this influence.

Concerning the Pan-African movement of W. E. B. DuBois, opinion in nationalist circles in English-speaking West Africa was generally a mixture of enthusiasm, mild criticism, and an attitude which implied that there was no direct rapport between DuBois' Pan-Africanism and the new pan-West African nationalism of the 1920s. It was a grand movement, to be admired and held up as an indication of a new and vigorous race-consciousness determined to assert itself in the post-war world, but was at the same time not directly related to peculiar economic and political problems of British West Africa. As far as Garvey's Pan-Negro movement was concerned, however, the position, contrary to the opinion of certain European contemporary writers, was different. As Thomas Hodgkin has suggested, the Garvey movement may have had a more significant and widespread effect on African nationalist thought than is commonly supposed. Professor Shepperson has already argued the thesis of Negro American influences on African nationalism, particularly East and Central African nationalism, although the extent and significance of this influence varied somewhat, as we shall show in the West African case. Some of the radical Negro newspapers found their way into Africa; for example, . . . an American writer, describing the network of influence linking Negroes throughout the world, wrote as follows: "Indeed, a reader in Sierra Leone writes to the *Negro World* (March 26, 1921): 'We have been reading the *Negro World* for about two years. We have been reading other Negro papers, such as the *New York Age*, the *Washington Bee*, the *Crisis*, the *Colored American*, the *Liberian West Africa*, the *Liberian Register*. . . .'"

Even as late as 1933 there were African nationalists in South Africa who, in spite of police surveillance, were receiving copies of Garvey's *Negro World*. One James Stehazu, for example (signing himself "Yours Africanly"), wrote to the *Negro World* editor "to express the feeling of our African brothers towards the American or West Indian brothers." His observations were frank and sharp:

> The Africans are now wide awake in affairs affecting the black races of the world, and yet the so-called civilized Negroes of the Western hemisphere are still permitting the white men to deceive them as the Negroes of the old régime, Uncle Tom stool-pigeons. If the "motherland" Africa is to be redeemed, the Africans are to play an important part in the ranks and file of the U.N.I.A. and A.C.L. I have studied comments and opinions of 29 leading American newspapers (all colored) and to my horror it is only one problem that is still harassing. The 250-year-old policy, "Please and Thank You" (Sir Kick Me and Thank You). But the lion-hearted M. Garvey has cut it adrift from the new

Negro. He is now admitted as a great African leader. . . . The intellectuals like Dr. DuBois, Pickens, Hancock and others are obviously put to shame, hopelessly moving like handicapped professors who are drunk with knowledge, who cannot help themselves. . . . The red, the black and the green are the colors talked about by the young men and women of Africa. It shall bury many and redeem millions. Today in Africa, the only hope of our race is gospel of U.N.I.A.—is sung and said as during the period of the French Revolution. . . .

While Garveyism did not have any permanent influence, the available evidence suggests that it excited more interest and controversy and was a more powerful utopia among African nationalist groups than the DuBoisian movement. In both French and British West Africa between 1920 and 1923, there were a few individuals and organizations associated with Garveyism. It was in Lagos, however, that the movement was strongest where a small but vigorous branch of U.N.I.A. was actually established in mid-1920, almost at the same time as the National Congress of British West Africa came into being. In March 1920, the Rev. Patriarch Campbell, one of the Congress leaders in Nigeria, was approached by some Lagosians on the subject of the Garvey movement and with a proposal for forming a committee of the U.N.I.A. in Lagos. Campbell advised them to postpone discussion until the meeting of the National Congress of British West Africa (hereafter referred to as N.C.B.W.A.) where he would take the matter up. He thought there was something to be said for the commercial aspects of Garvey's Pan-Negroism, especially the project of the Black Star Line, but advised loyal British subjects against participation in U.N.I.A. politics "as conditions in both hemispheres differ altogether from each other." Campbell then discussed the idea with delegates at the Accra meeting of the N.C.B.W.A. and the conclusion reached was that Garvey's politics should be ignored and the Black Star Line patronized, "it being a Negro undertaking and its object being solely for the purpose of facilitating and giving us more and brighter prospects as Africans in our commercial transactions." The *Times of Nigeria* editorial endorsed the view of the N.C.B.W.A., dwelling almost exclusively on the economic aspects of Garveyism.

The idea of establishing a line of steamers owned and controlled by Africans is a great and even sublime conception for which everybody of African origin will bless the name of Marcus Garvey. . . . The inclusion, however, of such a tremendous political plan, as the founding of a pan-African Empire, is too obviously ridiculous to do aught else than alienate sympathy from the whole movement. We do not suggest that our brethren in America ought not to aim at political autonomy. Liberty is man's highest right . . . particularly in the case of our American brethren, for whom the hardships and disadvantages under which they exist in the land of their exile make it desirable to have some portion of their ancestral land, where they could unmolested shape their own destiny and spread culture among their less enlightened brethren —"De ole folks at home."

The *Times* went on to argue, in a manner reminiscent of present Pan-African disagreements, that the N.C.B.W.A. concept of independence was incompatible with the U.N.I.A. concept of a Pan-Negro Republic: "If at all the day should come, and come it must in the process of evolution—when Africa shall be controlled by Africans, each distinct nation, while having the most cordial relations with every other sister nation, will infinitely prefer remaining as a separate political entity to being drawn into one huge melting pot of a Universal Negro Empire." The N.C.B.W.A. was cited as an example of a movement working towards the gradual independence of British West Africa within the British Empire, and Garvey was told that what Africa needed was banks, schools, industries, modern universities, and the Black Star Line, not "wild-cat schemes" like a Pan-African Republic. . . .

Apart from Liberia and Lagos, the U.N.I.A. does not seem to have had much impact on other parts of West Africa. Between 1920 and 1923 copies of the *Negro World* entered Dahomey via one of Quenum's sons in Paris, probably Kojo Tovalou Quenum who was associated with radical African groups in Paris. In the Senegal, Gambia, and Sierra Leone, governments introduced immigration restriction bills against "undesirables." Agents of U.N.I.A. appeared in Dakar (Senegal) but were expelled, as were those in Liberia. In the latter territory, U.N.I.A. made serious but abortive efforts at a colonization and trading scheme; their representatives arrived in Monrovia in January 1924, amply provided with funds to put before President King a scheme for the settlement of 3,000 Negroes from the United States. It was planned to establish six settlements of 500 families each, four on the French border and two on the British border. The Liberian President offered them an initial trial concession of 500 acres, but not on the border. The mission, however, failed, principally because of Garvey's intemperate attacks on the Liberian Government and his tactless criticism of the colonial powers. In the Senegal, a small group of Sierra Leoneans led by Francis Webber, Farmer, Dougherty, H. W. Wilson, and John Camara were preaching Garveyism. The British Consulate General in Dakar reported that the French authorities were "engaged in watching with some uneasiness the activities of a small group of men, natives of Sierra Leone, who were believed to be local representatives of the Universal Negro Improvement Association of the United States." The homes of these men were raided and documents seized; it was alleged that they had established at Rufisque "an active branch of the Association, provided with the usual elected officers, which branch was engaged in spreading the objects of the parent body and in collecting subscriptions for the furtherance of its schemes." John Camara was mentioned in the document as the U.N.I.A.'s "Travelling Commissioner" who visited most of the U.N.I.A. branches in West Africa in 1922, and in Dakar "meetings were held which were addressed by him in most violent language exhorting his hearers to spread the revolutionary movement which would, in the end, cast the white man out of Africa." In 1923, shortly before Garvey was imprisoned in the United States, an application by him to the British authorities for a passport to visit East Africa as part of his "speaking tour" of the world (to correct misrepresentations of the aims of U.N.I.A.) was refused by the Colonial Office on the ground that his visit might lead to more unrest. A Colonial Office despatch observed that "Marcus Garvey probably has a larger following in West Indies than he has in West Africa, but it is in Africa that he wants to institute his Negro State: consequently his object must be to stir up trouble and to incite sedition in Africa. What he wants from the West Indies is money. Probably that is his chief want so far as Africa is concerned as well; but if his movement is ever to achieve anything he must also create a spirit of unrest in Africa. . . ." Members of the Nigerian Executive Council unanimously advised against his visit, and importation of the *Negro World* was prohibited "as coming within the category of seditious, defamatory, scandalous or demoralising literature"; besides, his visit would be used "to collect further sums of money on false pretences from the most ignorant and gullible sections of the semi-educated Africans of the West Coast."

The admirers of Garvey, however, were not all "semi-educated," "ignorant and gullible." As M. Labouret argued in the 1930s, there were a few of the nationalist intelligentsia in British Africa who had studied Garveyism closely and had related it to nationalist politics. And it certainly comes as a surprise that the most outspoken and eloquent commentator on the Garvey movement among this intelligentsia was "that remarkable Cape Coast lawyer" (as Thomas Hodgkin rightly describes him), William Essuman Gwira Sekyi (or Kobina Sekyi), Gold Coast philosopher, nationalist, lawyer and traditionalist. A controversialist and prolific writer, Sekyi was one of the most interesting personalities in Gold Coast public affairs, and an example *par excellence*, of the African intellectual in nationalist politics. Sekyi devoted two interesting chapters to the Negro question in America in his violently anti-colonial book which recommended as little contact as possible between Africans and European colonials. Writing in defence of the Garvey movement he argued that any manifestation of solidarity between Africans and other Negroes was generally regarded with great suspicion by the white man who had "got so hopelessly alarmed by the *necessary spade-work* that Marcus Garvey is doing towards the erection, in the not very remote future of [an] abiding edifice of racial collaboration, that he has further overlooked the truth of the well-known remark: 'Abuse is no argument.' " . . . Unlike the majority of the Pan-African utopians, however, Sekyi was able to perceive that the African diaspora, for various historical and sociological reasons, had ceased to have any of the attributes of a nation and that West Indians and black Americans, in spite of the new race consciousness and Pan-Melanism, had inherited Anglo-Saxon prejudices against the African and were *ipso facto* disqualified from assuming any political leadership in the African continent:

> From Marcus Garvey's announcements regarding Africa, it is clear that he does not know even the level of acquaintance with Western ideals and of capacity to assimilate and adapt whatever comes from or is traceable to the modern world. What is much more important is that he does not understand how we Africans in Africa feel about such matters as the Colonial Government; neither can he and his set . . . realise that republican ideals in the crude form in which they are maintained, in theory, at least, in America go directly against the spirit of Africa, which is the only continent in the whole world peopled by human beings who have in their souls the secret of constitutional monarchy. . . . What Marcus Garvey and any other leader of Afro-American thought has first to appreciate before he can present a case sufficiently sound for Africa to support in the matter of combination or co-operation among all Africans at home and abroad, is the peculiar nature of the African standpoint in social and political institutions. *The salvation of the Africans in the world cannot but be most materially assisted by the Africans in America but must be controlled and directed from African Africa and thoroughly African Africans.* . . .

Garvey did not achieve the "great results" he hoped for, but to argue, as James Weldon Johnson did in *Black Manhattan,* that he was neither moderately successful nor successfully moderate, is to miss the point by judging him solely on the basis of immediate practical success. The political thought of great men does not have to be evaluated on the basis of the historian's success-story for its significance to be appreciated. As Samuel Butler has reminded us, "It is not he who first conceives an idea, nor he who sets it on its legs and makes it go on all fours, but he who makes other people accept the main conclusion, whether on right grounds or on wrong ones, who has done the greatest work as regards the promulgation of opinion." And this is what, in my view, Marcus Garvey did for Pan-Negro nationalism.

28

Rupert Lewis:
Garveyism in Jamaica[1]

Nowhere is the name of Marcus Garvey more revered today than in his native Jamaica, whose government after achieving independence from Great Britain proudly proclaimed him the island's first National Hero and now uses his portrait on its currency and postage stamps. Yet Garvey's activities in Jamaica both before and after the decade during which he lived in the United States have received comparatively little attention. Rupert Lewis, a young Jamaican scholar who teaches in the Department of Government of the University of the West Indies in Kingston, in this previously unpublished essay assesses the significance of Garvey's comprehensive reform program for Jamaica following his return to his homeland in 1927.

Marcus Garvey's deportation from the United States to Jamaica in November 1927 after being imprisoned for two years and nine months in the Atlanta Federal Prison was an important turning point in the struggle of our people against British colonialism. During 1916–27, while living and working in the United States, Garvey had become internationally known as the leader of the African struggle for self-determination.

His work, as was the case in many other parts of the world, had exerted a significant impact on the anti-colonial movement in the entire Caribbean area. Far from marking the end of his political life, his return to Jamaica on December 10, 1927, opened up a new phase of his work. This new phase saw Garvey involved in the formulation and defense of Jamaica's first anti-imperialist programme, organizing the island's first political party, trade union activities, municipal politics, the writing and staging of plays[2] at Edelweiss Park—the political

---

[1] "Garveyism in Jamaica," by Rupert Lewis. Copyright © 1973 by Rupert Lewis. This article appears in print for the first time. Used by permission of the author.

[2] Although none of his plays is known to have survived, Garvey wrote and produced at least four plays during these years in Jamaica: "The Coronation of an

154

and cultural headquarters of the Universal Negro Improvement Association and African Communities League and generally of the anti-colonial struggle in the country, the publication of two newspapers—*The Black Man* (1929–31) and the *New Jamaican* (1932–33), and organizing the Sixth (1929) and Seventh (1934) International Conventions of the UNIA in Kingston. In addition, in 1928 and 1931 he spent long periods in England and Western Europe agitating for the historic pan-African petition to the League of Nations which set out the conditions of the African people throughout the colonial world and called for self-determination. During the years 1935–40 Garvey also participated in the anti-fascist struggle in London against the barbaric Italian assault on Ethiopia.

This essay cannot discuss all these aspects of Marcus Garvey's work. It will instead briefly examine his political activities in Jamaica. Before this can be done, however, one needs to be aware of two things. Firstly, that the Garvey nationalist movement has to be seen as a part of the worldwide anti-imperialist upsurge which developed after the Russian Revolution of 1917 and World War I. Secondly, because the main area of imperialist penetration in Jamaica was agriculture, the national and racial question had at its core the decomposition of the peasantry into poor peasants, agricultural labourers, and a relatively privileged group of small proprietors who employed wage-labour but who were tied in numerous financial knots to the colonial state machine and the large landowners. A very small section of this stratum supported Garvey's anti-colonial programme; however, within Jamaica his movement was based on the broad mass of working people.

Commenting on Garvey's return to Jamaica, the island's leading colonial daily newspaper, the *Gleaner,* noted that "no denser crowd has ever been witnessed in Kingston. . . ." This enthusiastic mass response was a source of great concern to the colonial officials. In January, 1928, Garvey contemplated a tour of the Caribbean before going on to Europe to petition the League of Nations. This tour was not possible, for in addition to having been banned from the United States, where his support was strongest, Amy Jacques Garvey recalls that "none of the consuls for the Central American countries would vise his passport for entry." This was a severe blow, as the UNIA in these areas, organised primarily among West Indian migrant workers, was second in strength only to the North American divisions. The pro-American government of Cuba went furthest in enacting anti-Garvey legislation by banning the *Negro World* newspaper in 1928 and declaring the UNIA an illegal organization in 1929. Due to vig-

African King" (1930), "Roaming Jamaicans" (1930), "Slavery: From Hut to Mansion" (1930), and "Wine, Women, and War" (1932).

orous protests, this ban on the UNIA ended after twenty-six weeks, after which time the Liberty Halls in Cuba were once more reopened but under strict surveillance. However, the Cuban government banned Garvey from entering the country. He was also prohibited from visiting other West Indian islands and Guyana.

In Trinidad there was a vigorous anti-Garvey lobby among certain school-teachers who in their journal argued against his visit. Their publication agreed with the colonial government that Marcus Garvey should be banned because "his presence will simply upset the peace and harmony which at present obtain among the various races in the colony. . . ."

This was typical of the colonial outlook of the black small proprietor class in the British West Indian colonies. This emergent middle class grew out of the decomposition of the peasantry and was supplemented by teachers, policemen, lawyers, junior civil servants, and a few technical people which the Crown colony system required for administrative purposes. British colonialism literally nurtured this "native" middle class. So while this class had a relatively strong nationalist outlook in Egypt, China, and India because of a different history and relationship to imperialism, in Jamaica and the West Indies it acted more often as a brake on the anti-imperialist movement once its narrow constitutional demands were met. Generally, this class could not imagine a future in which British capitalism did not play an important role in the country's life.

After returning from his lengthy working tour of Western Europe and Canada, in November, 1928, Garvey immediately launched the People's Political Party at a mass rally attended by 5,000 people. By the end of March, 1929, he had begun publication of the daily *Black Man* newspaper, the first daily newspaper in the history of the press in the country to represent uncompromisingly the oppressed African majority. This newspaper served not only as the organ of the local UNIA, thereby complementing the American *Negro World,* but also was one of the main vehicles of the political programme of the PPP. The paper's policy statement read in part:

> As the independent tribune of an oppressed people, the "Black Man" records conditions affecting the Negro masses throughout the world. Its function embraces the exposé and remedy of the terrorism and injustice to which the Negro is subjected. Its scope is international. From the remote corners of Seni Gambia, Senegal and the Congo, it catches the cry of benighted tribesmen suffering by the hand of ruthless despoilers and carries it to the scattered millions of black men and women in Europe, the United States and the West Indies.

More than ever black people needed such a newspaper. The exploitation and oppression of colonial peoples had been intensified by an acute international capitalist crisis during 1930–33, called the "Depression." Unemployment in the capitalist world rose to 35 million, while in the colonies it meant that the prices received for agricultural raw materials and food dropped considerably in value on the world market. This meant that the imperialists increased their plunder of the peasants' land in the colonies, which was seized by large landowners and avaricious creditors. Moreover, between 1930–34 over 30,000 migrants from the United States and Central America returned to Jamaica to live in further misery.

Even before the Depression, Garvey's second petition to the League of Nations in 1928 had eloquently described the erosion of civil liberties and of living conditions of African people throughout the world. The sections dealing with the proletarianisation of the peasantry, the treatment of African mine workers, and the pass laws of South Africa destroy the myth that he had only a vague and romantic notion of African reality. The petition also protested restrictions on immigration and emigration, the non-issuance of passports, non-accommodation on steamships, and other barriers to travel by blacks. The Depression brought not only worsening economic conditions but further racial and national oppression of black people. It also stimulated a resurgence of the anti-colonial mass movement which had dominated Jamaican political life in the years immediately after World War I.

Marcus Garvey paid special attention to the upsurge of the anti-colonial movement in other parts of the British Empire, in Ireland, Africa and Asia. In commenting on the Indian nationalist struggle he wrote:

> Today the whole world is attracted to the movement of that wonderful man on India—Mahatma Gandhi—who has for several weeks been on the march through India toward a given point, arousing his countrymen to the consciousness of national independence. . . . The Indians are an oppressed race—oppressed by some of their own as well as by external forces. Like the Negro they must struggle upward to justify their national existence, and so Gandhi is leading and pointing the way. . . .

Garvey not only defended the national liberation movements in Morocco, India, Ireland and Egypt against the many attacks in the colonial press, but pointed out:

> We, who are Africans, at home and abroad, have hopes of the future, and so we watch, with a friendly eye, the activities in India, because after India may come Africa.

It is important to emphasize that the Garvey movement constituted a part of this larger movement against colonial domination throughout the world. The historic 1929 manifesto of the People's Political Party summed up briefly and clearly the major economic, political, legal, and educational demands of the Jamaican working people. It was on that basis that Garvey waged an intensive campaign against British colonial rule and the big landowners and merchants. This programme formed the basis of his work in Jamaica and showed his practical and realistic approach to politics.

First, let us list the economic demands:

1. Protection of native labour.
2. A minimum wage for the labouring and working classes of the island.
3. A law to protect the working and labouring classes of the country by insurance against accident, sickness, and death occurring during employment.
4. An eight hour working day throughout Jamaica.
5. Land reform.
6. A law to encourage the promotion of native industries.
7. A law to compel the employment of not less than 60 percent of native labour in all industrial, agricultural, and commercial activities in Jamaica.
8. The establishment by the Government of an electrical system to supply cheap electricity to such growing and prospering centres as are necessary.
9. The compulsory improvement of urban areas from which large profits are made by trusts, corporations, combines and companies.
10. A law to prevent criminal profiteering in the sale of lands in urban and suburban areas to the detriment of the expansion of healthy home life of citizens of moderate means—profiteering such as has occurred in lower St. Andrew by heartless land sharks.
11. A law to empower the Parochial boards of each parish to undertake, under the direction of the Central Government, the building of model sanitary homes for the peasantry by a system of easy payments over a period of from ten to twenty years.
12. A law to empower the Government to secure a loan of three million (or more) pounds from the Imperial government, or otherwise, to be used by the Government, under the management of a department of the Director of Agriculture in developing the Crown lands of the island, agriculturally and other-

wise, with the object of supplying employment for our surplus unemployed population and to find employment for stranded Jamaicans abroad; and that the Government purchase such ships as are necessary from time to time, to facilitate the marketing of the produce gathered from these Crown lands, and at the same time offering an opportunity to other producers to ship and market their produce.

This last plank cannot, of course, be separated from the demand for land reform. Twelve of Garvey's twenty-six planks in his manifesto dealt with basic economic problems.

On the question of political self-determination, Garvey argued that in 1930, given the point that had been reached by nationalist struggles of other colonial people within the British Empire, "a larger modicum of self-government" was possible on the road towards political independence. Self-rule was the long term objective of the 1920 "Declaration of Rights of the Negro Peoples of the World." This is the context in which Garvey called for legal and prison reform. In one of his planks he demanded a "law to impeach and imprison judges who, with disregard for British justice and constitutional rights, dealt unfairly." For this plank Garvey was tried for contempt of court, sentenced to three months imprisonment, and fined 200 Jamaican dollars. He had to serve the sentence and pay the fine. The white judges saw this as an affront to their domination of the judiciary and a challenge to the entire legal basis of Crown Colony rule. They therefore dealt with Garvey ruthlessly. Garvey's platform also included demands for proper medical services for the masses, the establishment of a university, a polytechnic, high schools and technical institutes in every parish, public libraries, and a National Opera House with an Academy of Music.

Garvey defended this far-reaching programme by contending that within the context of colonial domination the democratic struggle for greater economic, political, civil, and cultural liberties would provide the preconditions for the further advance of the African people toward full freedom. The defeat of Garvey himself and most of his candidates in the January 1930 election to the Legislative Council was due, firstly, to the fact that the masses had no vote. Secondly, the big landowners, merchants, and the colonial officials had won the support of the small proprietor class—i.e., farmers, produce-dealers, inspectors, parsons, teachers, policemen, and shopkeepers—in the urban and rural areas.

However, electoral defeat did not mean the end of Garvey's programme. Throughout his years in Jamaica he pressed for these demands through workers' associations, the Municipal Council, the

UNIA, and his newspapers. Garvey's political activities in Jamaica between 1929 and 1935 should be seen in light of his statement that "To fight for African redemption does not mean that we must give up our domestic fights for political justice and industrial rights." His work and ideas were the basis for later Jamaican advances. It is precisely these struggles for political justice and economic rights, such as Marcus Garvey's campaign in Jamaica in the early 1930's, which pave the way for the broader struggle against the exploitation of imperialism and which make the goal of "the redemption of Africa" and black liberation realistic and possible.

29

The Republic of Cameroon: An African Tribute[1]

Perhaps the best evidence of Marcus Garvey's influence on African nationalism is the growing recognition by present-day Africans of his prominent role in the struggle for African freedom. As the first prime minister of newly independent Ghana, Kwame Nkrumah prominently displayed a portrait of Garvey in his office and freely acknowledged his debt to Garvey's Philosophy and Opinions, *which he read while a student in the United States in the late 1930s. It was no accident that, once in power, Nkrumah quickly established a Ghanaian steamship company named the Black Star Line. Other African leaders and nations have paid similar tributes to Garvey. In 1969 the Federal Republic of Cameroon issued a postage stamp in his honor for reasons explained in the following letter to Garvey's widow.*

TO MRS. AMY JACQUES GARVEY

Yaounde, 21 November 1969

Dear Madam,

I have the honour and pleasure to forward to you herewith commemorative stamps and envelopes of the first day of issue in honour of six prominent Negro Writers, among whom is your celebrated husband, Marcus Garvey.

As you know only too well, the collection of his writings compiled by yourself under the title of "The Philosophy & Opinions of Marcus Garvey" had a great impact on the movement for African independence and Negro freedom.

Marcus Garvey died almost thirty years ago, but his spirit is still marching on, as witnessed by the resurgence of the Negro self-assertion that is sweeping through the United States today, and by the independence and the consolidation of Black Power in Africa.

[1] From Dr. Bernard Fonlon (Yaounde) to Amy Jacques Garvey (Kingston), November 21, 1969, original in possession of Mrs. Garvey. Reprinted by permission of Amy Jacques Garvey.

We are glad and proud that the Federal Republic of Cameroon is the first country ever to honour prominent Negro writers in this way.

I am forwarding also, under separate cover, another set for Marcus Garvey, Junior. Hoping that this gesture will give you as much joy as it has been to us.

Dr. Bernard Fonlon
Minister of Transport, Posts and Telecommunication.

30
Clarence Harding:
Continuing Garvey's Work
in Africa[1]

*Garvey's dream for the redemption of Africa was predi-
cated on the hope that the Republic of Liberia, at the time the
only independent black African nation, would be available as a
base of U.N.I.A. operations. As we have seen, his plans were frustrated, however, when British and French pressure led the Liberian government to expel the advance party of Garveyites in
1924, thereby effectively ending any Back to Africa movement for
the liberation of the African motherland. Recently the revived
Universal Negro Improvement Association launched another,
more successful venture in Liberia. Under the leadership of
U.N.I.A. High Commissioner Clarence Harding, a Chicago-born
clergyman, the Marcus Garvey Memorial Institute was established
in Monrovia in 1967 to provide education at several levels and
especially to teach the pan-African philosophy of Garveyism. The
following interview with Commissioner Harding about the work
of the Garvey Institute was conducted by Bro. Ruwa Chiri, a
Chicago writer and poet, on the occasion of Rev. Harding's return visit to the United States after five years of service in Liberia.*

Bro. Ruwa: You mentioned the U.A.I.A. and that's something
that a lot of people, at least younger people who have grown up in
the post World War II era, think is perhaps buried in black history
books. . . .

Comm. Harding: Well, the U.A.I.A.—We use the term U.A.I.A. to
mean the Universal Afrikan Improvement Association. The original
name is the Universal Negro Improvement Association. The Afrikan
does not, and will not accept the term "Negro" as such. So, by the con-

[1] "Interview with the Reverend Clarence Harding," *Afrika Must Unite*, March–
April, 1972, pp. 5–6, 10, 13–14. Reprinted by permission of Amy Jacques Garvey,
the Reverend Clarence Harding, and Thomas Harvey, President General, U.N.I.A.

sent of the International convention we substituted the word Afrikan. The U.A.I.A. or the U.N.I.A. is nothing more than the Garvey Movement, and it is not only alive, but kicking lustily, still on the battlefields for Afrikan freedom. . . .

Bro. Ruwa: What are some of the things that it is doing?

Comm. Harding: In Afrika today we maintain a medical project and an agricultural project. We maintain the Garvey Memorial Institute which consists of three schols; an elementary school, a junior high school and a senior high school. We are hoping to open a junior college if support warrants it.

Bro. Ruwa: When was the Marcus Garvey Memorial Institute founded?

Comm. Harding: The Garvey Memorial Institute was founded approximately five years ago, in January 1967. We had preliminary classes in '66. It became a regular institute for training in '67.

Bro. Ruwa: Could you give us an idea of some of the programs that the Marcus Garvey Memorial Institute is involved in?

Comm. Harding: Well, one of the things we are laying emphasis on is Afrikan studies. But, we have the same things that we have here: Math, Science, Social Studies and Language Arts. However, we emphasize Afrikan studies. The projection of the Afrikan image, workshops on the nations that make up the Afrikan continent. We try to let our students know who are the heads of the Afrikan states, how they are governed, what is their national product (GNP), how important they are to Afrikan unity: to teach the student what Afrikan unity really means and what functional global Black unity really means. These are some of the focuses we have.

Bro. Ruwa: In other words, the movement, the Marcus Garvey Movement is still talking about "Afrika for the Afrikans."

Comm. Harding: They are not talking, they are doing. . . .

Bro. Ruwa: How could we, the present day Pan-Afrikans hook up internationally? We know that this was, perhaps, one of Marcus Garvey's greatest contributions. This "noble" idea of moving masses of Black people around the world as he did in his time. How should we carry on this work?

Comm. Harding: I think we should carry it on by creating institutions on the continent that are mass-oriented. I do not think that you can do much of anything through any existing Afrikan governments. Afrikan governments who would otherwise cooperate, by reason of their economic entanglement with Europe, cannot come out and officially say so. The Black man, the Black woman, the Black child has a role to play in Afrika. It can be played by bringing about the concept among all Afrikan people, that they are one, and mass movements under that official level should be their focus. When we get enough masses, enough people, no matter what the language is or no matter what the customs are, speaking and being aware that there is a oneness, being aware that we should be one, not only spiritually, but politically, then those pressures will begin to build up and governments will have to react to the demands of their own people. Then we will have good Afrikan unity. The loose form, such as we have as represented by the O.A.U. must begin to talk in terms of an all Afrikan party that would have certain legislative powers.

Bro. Ruwa: Talking about the O.A.U., some critics, maybe a little bit acidly, have characterized the O.A.U. as the N.A.A.C.P. of Afrika. Is that fair criticism?

Comm. Harding: I would rather think so. I know this is something we don't want to say, but it needs to be said. When Dr. Nkrumah was active in the O.A.U. it had backbone and it could always be looked forward to for some positive action. Since Dr. Nkrumah is no longer a part of it, it seems to have lost its soul and it has become a debating society, something that goes through the motions of mouthing Afrikan freedom, but nothing more. The liberation committee whose sole function was to challenge and study the liberation movements; to find out what help is needed and to give that help, has become a political football, a source of outright graft for certain unscrupulous persons whom the O.A.U. has appointed to represent it in Dar Es Salaam and other revolutionary headquarters. So much so that the government of that particular country protested. Julius Nyerere said that he was tired of bearing the responsibility of the liberation movement, which Tanzania has done in a large measure, while other Afrikan countries just talk.

Bro. Ruwa: How does modern Garveyism view the liberation movement in Guinea-Bissau, Angola, and Zimbabwe, etc?

Comm. Harding: Well, the modern Garvey Movement view is the same as the not-so-modern Garvey Movement: Any time Black people are struggling for freedom anywhere in the world, they should have the sympathy and support of Black people elsewhere in the world. We endorse it 100%. We regret that the support is not forthcoming. . . .

Bro. Ruwa: A final question would be concerning where you are from.

Comm. Harding: I have lived in Chicago many years. I was born in Chicago and I was one of the associate directors of the anti-poverty program for the City of Chicago. In that capacity I was able to know just what conditions face the majority of our people. It disgusted me and I figured that the only true seat of black power was in Afrika.

The only aggressive thing that could be done for our people would ultimately have to be done in Afrika. The bloodshed and all of the things we have experienced here have been futile.

Bro. Ruwa: Your leaving Chicago and going to Afrika to work brings up a much debated question wherein a lot of Black people in the United States claim that going to Afrika or working for Pan-Afrikanism or working to redeem Black people around the world, is a form of "copout" from the struggle in this country. How do you respond to that?

Comm. Harding: I think, let everyone be of his own opinion. The people who have worked—for instance, I have done my share in this country. I was a freedom fighter before it became popular. I have been to jail, I have been to all of those kinds of things as a minister and as a civil servant. I participated in brawls with the local police. We integrated restaurants and businesses and the usual stuff that was so popular here a few years ago. After doing all that we found that the movement's fate was integration. The white man was able to reach them in some kind of way. They either employ the leadership or destroy the leadership. The masses were right back to the same position as they were before. Of course, there were some gains; the spirit of rebellion was kindled. But, we held, and I hold, that someone had to go to prepare a place: That when the Black man's position in the western world becomes untenable he would have a sanctuary strong enough and powerful enough to defend him. He could come home, feel at home, and take his place there among the nations and people of the earth as he should.

Bro. Ruwa: You are again saying what the critics of Pan-Afrikanism say will never happen. Are you saying that the Black man's position in this country will become untenable at some point?

Comm. Harding: Yes.

Bro. Ruwa: How is that? It hasn't become untenable in four hundred years.

Comm. Harding: Hasn't it? Then why are we still protesting? Most people's struggle is marked by one single incident or two or three incidents, some perhaps bloody, but there is usually one final way. We are still going on; still begging to be tolerated by white people. We are still trying to give him a report card as to what great things we have done for America because we want to stay here. We want to be wanted; to be with him, to be a part of his society to the detriment and death of our own culture. . . .

Afterword: An Enduring Legacy

Although the Garvey movement had seemingly disintegrated as an organized force by the time of its leader's death in 1940, Marcus Garvey's ideas and example have remained a potent and enduring legacy. Increasingly in the years after World War II there developed in the black world a renewed interest in Garvey's black nationalist philosophy. As new black nations emerged one by one in Africa in the 1950s and 1960s, as his homeland of Jamaica received its independence and experimented briefly with a federated union with other black West Indies island states, and as militant black power leaders of the civil rights movement in the United States (some of them, like Malcolm X, the children of Garveyites) began again to stress racial pride and separatism, Garvey seemed thoroughly vindicated. Indeed, as we have seen, three decades after his death his revitalized Universal Negro Improvement Association was still carrying on the struggle for black liberation and African redemption in cooperation with other Garvey-inspired black nationalist groups. And only a few miles from Garvey's old headquarters in Harlem there was official recognition of his work; in response to a vote by local residents, the New York City Housing Authority in 1972 named a large urban renewal housing project in Brooklyn the Marcus Garvey Park Village. The reawakened interest in Garveyism extended throughout the black world, including the African motherland, which Garvey, much to his regret, never saw. Appropriately, one of the first acts of newly independent Ghana was to establish a national steamship company named the Black Star Line.

Garvey's triumph was most notable in his native Jamaica, however. Once scorned by the Jamaican power structure, Garvey is today regarded in his island homeland as a black George Washington, the father of Jamaican independence. Streets are named after him; his bust is prominently displayed in a park in the capital city of Kingston; his portrait appears on the currency and postage stamps. In 1964 the Jamaican government brought his remains home from an obscure London grave and proudly placed them in a Marcus Garvey National Shrine. Garvey was officially designated Jamaica's first National Hero, with his birthday, August 17, henceforth to be celebrated appropriately. In 1968, on the twentieth anniversary of the adoption of the United Nations Declaration on Human Rights, a document embodying many of the ideas included in the 1920 U.N.I.A. declaration,

Jamaica awarded a special £5,000 Marcus Garvey Prize for Human Rights posthumously to the martyred Martin Luther King, Jr., who in a different way had come closer to equaling Garvey's inspirational hold over the black masses in America than any other race leader since his day. All in all, this was impressive if belated recognition for a native son who had spent the last five years of his life in voluntary exile following his political rebuffs and the collapse of his efforts to rebuild his movement from a base in his homeland.

Garvey's striking success in organizing the first truly mass movement among American Negroes, and one with a significant international character as well, was a remarkable achievement. Whatever the precise membership of the Universal Negro Improvement Association in its heyday—and the estimates vary widely—there were surely millions of blacks in the United States and throughout the world who followed Garvey's activities closely and who thrilled at his stirring call for a rebirth of the race. Who could fail to be moved by the audacity of his dreams, his inspired oratory, his account of past glories, and his vision of future greatness? Garvey appeared fortuitously at a time when the Negro masses were awaiting a black Moses, and he became the instrument through which they could express their longings and deep discontent. The current of black nationalism which he helped to set in motion has not yet run its course, for, as one of his followers once boasted, Marcus Garvey opened windows in the minds of Negroes. By any measure, here was one of the most interesting and influential figures of the twentieth century.

And yet, for all his daring, driving energy, and impressive organizational skill, in many respects Garvey remains a controversial and even tragic figure. Like a meteor streaking across the black sky, his star flamed brightly for a moment and then quickly burned out. For all practical purposes his movement lasted scarcely a decade. Personally honest, dedicated, and sincere, he raised more money in a brief period than any previous black leader. Yet these funds were never equal to his ambitious plans, and blundering mismanagement fatally weakened his commercial uplift ventures, such as the ill-conceived Black Star Line. Having invested his life and all available resources in the movement, Garvey died penniless, leaving his widow nothing but proud memories with which to raise their two young sons. By then little remained of the Universal Negro Improvement Association but memories. As Ralph Bunche has remarked, "When the curtain dropped on the Garvey theatricals, the black man of America was exactly where Garvey had found him, though a little bit sadder, perhaps a bit poorer—if not wiser." [1]

[1] Quoted in Gunnar Myrdal, *An American Dilemma: the Negro Problem and Modern Democracy* (New York: Harper, 1944), p. 748.

This assessment is incomplete, for Garvey's chief legacy, and an important one, was spiritual rather than organizational. He helped to give Negroes everywhere a new feeling of racial pride and a confidence in their collective and individual worth. He made the black masses proud of their past and resolute to face the future. His black nationalist ideas continue to have great appeal and lasting influence. To be sure, not all blacks (nor, for that matter, many whites) were then or are today prepared to concede Garvey's assumption that a black minority could never hope to achieve justice and full equality in a white-dominated society such as the United States. But he forced blacks and whites alike to reexamine the realities of American democracy and to face up to its shortcomings. Any substantial Back-to-Africa movement under U.N.I.A. auspices was as visionary and impractical as the colonization schemes for Liberia and Sierra Leone of the nineteenth century, because few American Negroes were interested in a "return" to a land they had never known. Yet there is no denying the success and value of Garvey's efforts to rekindle among the Negroes of the New World an interest in their African roots. The great proliferation of Negro history courses and African and black studies programs in American schools and colleges in recent years is a measure of the ready acceptance of this aspect of his philosophy today. Marcus Garvey, it seems abundantly clear, will continue to play a significant role in the struggle for the liberation of black people. Nothing could have pleased him more, for as he had once told his followers:

> When I am dead wrap the mantle of the Red, Black and Green around me, for in the new life I shall rise with God's grace and blessing to lead the millions up the heights of triumph with the colors that you well know. Look for me in the whirlwind or the storm, look for me all around you, for, with God's grace, I shall come and bring with me countless millions of black slaves who have died in America and the West Indies and the millions in Africa to aid you in the fight for Liberty, Freedom and Life.[2]

[2] Amy Jacques Garvey, ed., *Philosophy and Opinions of Marcus Garvey*, vol. II (New York: Universal Publishing House, 1926), p. 239. Reprinted by permission of Amy Jacques Garvey.

Bibliographical Note

Garvey wrote prolifically about his movement and his black nationalist philosophy, but little about his own life. The closest thing to an autobiography was his article "The Negro's Greatest Enemy," *Current History Magazine* 18 (September, 1923): 951–57. Many of Garvey's editorials, speeches, manifestoes, and accounts of his activities are to be found in the scattered files of the periodicals he published: the weekly *Negro World* (New York, 1918–33), the daily *Negro Times* (New York, 1922–23), the daily *Black Man* (Jamaica, 1929–31), the daily *New Jamaican* (Jamaica, 1932–33), and the monthly *Black Man* (London, 1935–39?). His widow, Amy Jacques Garvey, edited two volumes of his early writings, *Philosophy and Opinions of Marcus Garvey* (New York: Universal Publishing House, 1923) and *Philosophy and Opinions of Marcus Garvey: Or Africa for the Africans* (New York: Universal Publishing House, 1926). Since the second of these books was published as Volume II, despite its longer title, both works are cited here as Volumes I and II of the *Philosophy and Opinions of Marcus Garvey*. Volume II also contains the autobiographical *Current History* article cited above. Long out of print and extremely rare, both volumes of the *Philosophy and Opinions* were recently reprinted in the United States and England (London: Cass, 1967; New York: Arno Press, 1968–69). Mrs. Garvey also edited two volumes of her husband's poetry, *The Tragedy of White Injustice* and *Selections from the Poetic Meditations of Marcus Garvey* (New York: Amy Jacques Garvey, 1927), and a pamphlet dealing with his trial and conviction, *United States of America vs. Marcus Garvey: Was Justice Defeated?* (New York: Amy Jacques Garvey, 1925). Several of Garvey's speeches were published in pamphlet form: *Speech of Marcus Garvey . . . Delivered at 71st Regiment Armory* (n.d.); *Speech at Madison Square Garden on the Return of a Delegation from Abroad* (New York, 1924); *Aims and Objects of Movement for Solution of Negro Problem Outlined* (New York: U.N.I.A., 1924); *Speech Delivered by Marcus Garvey at Royal Albert Hall, London* (London: U.N.I.A., 1928); *Minutes of Proceedings of a Speech by Marcus Garvey at the Century Theatre, London, Sunday, September 2, 1928* (London: Vail, 1928). Both the 1922 and 1928 appeals to the League of Nations are included in *Renewal of Petition of the Universal Negro Improvement Association and African Communities League to the League of Nations* (London: Vail, 1928).

Unfortunately, Garvey's papers apparently did not survive his many moves, his imprisonment, and the London bombings in 1940–41 following his death. In 1970 a collection of U.N.I.A. organizational records was discovered in an abandoned building in Harlem, and although a dispute ensued over ownership, a substantial part of the papers was deposited in the Schomburg Collection of the Harlem branch of the New York Public Library. Other valuable material about the Black Star Line, Garvey's activities and influence abroad, and the abortive U.N.I.A. colonization venture in Liberia is to be found in the archives of the Department of State and the United States Shipping Board, both in the National Archives. There are original Black Star Line papers in the files of the United States District Court for the Southern District of New York, *U.S.* v. *Marcus Garvey*, dockets C31-37 and C33-688, and the record of Garvey's income tax case is contained in docket C38-771. More important is the printed record of his federal mail fraud trial, *Marcus Garvey* v. *U.S.*, United States Circuit Court of Appeals, Second Circuit, docket 8317, which contains detailed testimony and several hundred government and defense exhibits about the Black Star Line and larger aspects of the U.N.I.A. movement. Mrs. Amy Jacques Garvey has a good deal of Garvey material in her possession, and she and Richard Hart have helped to build the Garvey collection of the West Indies Reference Library of the Institute of Jamaica.

The American Negro press was largely hostile to Garvey but followed his activities closely. The *Chicago Defender* was perhaps his most consistent critic in the years 1920–27, but the New York *Age,* the New York *Amsterdam News,* the Washington *Bee,* the Pittsburgh *Courier,* and the Baltimore *Afro-American* also gave generally critical coverage of Garvey's activities. Dr. W. E. B. DuBois, the scholarly editor of *Crisis,* the organ of the National Association for the Advancement of Colored People, wrote several devastating critiques of the Garvey movement. Other important black periodicals which sometimes criticized Garveyism include: *Messenger,* which spearheaded the "Garvey Must Go" campaign; the Marxist *Liberator* and *Crusader;* *Challenge;* and *Spokesman.* For a time the Garvey-inspired African Orthodox Church published the *Negro Churchman.* The Kingston *Gleaner* gave thorough coverage of Garvey's activities in Jamaica following his deportation from the United States in 1927 and is the best source on the renewed interest in Garvey in Jamaica since World War II. Interesting attempts to revive Garveyism following the founder's death may be found in such periodicals as the *New Negro World,* the *Voice of Freedom,* the *African, Abeng, Bongo-Man,* the *Blackman, Afrika Must Unite,* and *Tom-Tom.*

The first book-length biography of Garvey appeared in the year of his death; written by a Jamaican journalist, Len S. Nembhard, it is titled *Trials and Triumphs of Marcus Garvey* (Kingston: Gleaner, 1940). The Nembhard work was popular in nature, laudatory, and emphasized Garvey's activities in Jamaica following his deportation from America. E. David Cronon published a scholarly biography fifteen years later under the title *Black Moses: the Story of Marcus Garvey and the Universal Negro Improvement Association* (Madison: University of Wisconsin Press, 1955, reprinted with new preface, 1969), which has gone through numerous printings and has remained a standard reference work. Amy Jacques Garvey's *Garvey and Garveyism* (Kingston: Amy Jacques Garvey, 1963), is part biography, part autobiographical reminiscence, and adds new details about Garvey's personality and family life, especially for the period of the late 1920s and 1930s. Mrs. Garvey's *Black Power in America: Marcus Garvey's Impact on Jamaica and Africa: the Power of the Human Spirit* (Kingston: Amy Jacques Garvey, 1968), gives additional information about Garvey's activities in the United States and Jamaica, as well as about his influence in Africa. Theodore G. Vincent's *Black Power and the Garvey Movement* (Berkeley: Ramparts Press [1971]), as its title suggests, is as much a plea for contemporary black power ideas as it is a chronicle of the Garvey movement, though Vincent has also added to our knowledge of Garvey and the U.N.I.A. in his diffuse and poorly organized book. Another recent biography is Elton C. Fax's *Garvey: the Story of a Pioneer Black Nationalist* (New York: Dodd, Mead, 1972), which also contains a helpful introduction by John Henrik Clarke. Garvey inspired numerous articles discussing his program and philosophy during his life, as well as others of increasing frequency and interpretive quality since his death. Excerpts from some of these articles are included in Parts Two and Three of this book.

Index

Abbott, Robert S., 43
Advertising, 5, 43, 45
Africa Times and Orient Review, 2
African Legion, 8, 73, 132, 133
African Orthodox Church, 9, 73, 107, 132
African redemption, program of, 8–9, 47–50, 53–55, 64, 70–71, 86–87, 94–95, 125–27, 131–34, 141–53, 161–69
Afro-American, 44
Aldred, Amy, 25
Alexander, Lewis, 128
American Colonization Society, 125
American Expeditionary Force, 4
Anglo-Saxon Clubs of America, 60, 97, 99
Angola, 165
"Appeal to the Soul of White America" (Garvey), 99
Ashwood, Amy, 25
Atlanta Penitentiary, 13, 61

Bagnall, Robert W., 102–6, 129
Barclay, Edwin J., 9
Basutoland, 94–95
Belgian Congo, 90
Bibliographical note, 170–72
Bilbo, Theodore G., 70–71, 135–40
Birbeck College, London, 2
Black Cross Navigation and Trading Company, 12, 67, 133
Black Cross Nurses, 8, 120, 132
Black Man, 15, 69, 155, 156
Black Manhattan (Johnson), 123–25, 153
Black Star Line, 6–7, 10–12, 20, 25–26, 47, 61–64, 76, 78, 80–87, 102, 104–6, 127, 132, 139, 150, 168
Black Star Line (Ghana), 146, 161, 167
Black Star Steamship Company, 11, 74, 90
Bluefield's Messenger, 80
Booker T. Washington (ship), 12, 13
Bratton, Bishop, 108
Brisbane, Robert Hughes, Jr., 126–29
Brown, T. T., 24

Buell, R. L., 145
Bunche, Ralph, 168
Butler, Samuel, 153

Camara, John, 93, 151, 152
Cameroon, Federal Republic of, 161–62
Campbell, Gwen., 25
Campbell, Rev. Patriarch, 150
Cary, Joyce, 89–91
Case for African Freedom, The (Cary), 89–91
Chicago Defender, 43, 44, 45, 54
Chronology, 17–18
Cockbourne, Joshua, 6
Coleman, James, 143
Colored American, 149
"Committee of Eight," 102
Communism, 57–59, 112–17
Congo, 145
Congressional Record, 135–40
Coolidge, Calvin, 13, 61, 115, 139
Cox, Ernest Sevier, 97–99, 116, 136, 138
Crisis, The, 80, 130, 131, 149
Cross, Robert, 25
Cuba, 155–56
Curzon, Lord, 92

Dahomey, 151
Daily, Adrian A., 24
Dakar, French West Africa, 92–93, 151
Daugherty, Harry M., 102
"Death or a Program!" (Minor), 112–17
Declaration of the Rights of the Negro Peoples of the World, 8–9, 30–37, 89–91, 145, 159
Demetrius of Ephesus, 108–9
Dimon, C. L., 84
Disraeli, Benjamin, 49
Dorsinville, Luc, 105
Dougherty, 93, 151
Du Bois, W. E. B., 51, 54–56, 66–67, 80–88, 102, 104, 119, 124, 130–34, 144–47, 149

Duse Mohammed Ali, 2
Dyer, Stienbart, 59, 136

Egypt, 157
Essien-Udom, E. U., 148
Ethiopia, 69, 155

Farmer, 93, 151
Firestone, Harvey, 115
Firestone Tire & Rubber Company, 13, 115, 138
Fonlon, Bernard, 161–62
France, 13, 55, 87, 92–93, 150–52
Frazier, E. Franklin, 118–22

Gambia, 93, 151
Gandhi, Mahatma, 157
Garvey, Amy Jacques, 13, 19, 27, 30, 38, 43, 47, 51, 57, 61, 67, 97, 107, 121, 146, 155, 161–62, 168, 169
Garvey, Marcus (father), 1, 20
Garvey, Marcus Mosiah
    African Orthodox Church, 9, 107, 132
    African redemption, program of, 8–9, 47–50, 53–55, 64, 70–71, 86–87, 94–95, 125–27, 131–34, 141–53, 161–69
    ancestry, 1
    birth, 1
    Black Cross Navigation and Trading Company, 12, 67, 133
    Black Man, 15, 69, 155, 156–57
    Black Star Line, 6–7, 10–12, 20, 25–26, 61–64, 80–87, 104–6, 132, 139
    Black Star Steamship Company, 11, 74, 90
    childhood, 20–22
    on Communism, 57–59
    death, 16
    deportation, 14, 61, 139
    Du Bois and, 54–56, 66–67, 80–88, 102, 124, 130–34, 144–47
    early employment, 2
    education, 1–2, 20–21
    in Jamaica, 1–3, 14–15, 69, 80–81, 154–60
    Ku Klux Klan and, 59–60, 97, 116–17
    labor unions, 2, 57–59
    League of Nations, petitions to, 14, 155, 157
    in London, 2–3, 15–16, 69, 155
    marriage, 82
    as mass leader, 118–22, 124
    maxims, 27–29
    Negro Factories Corporation, 7
        on Negro press, 43–46
        Negro World, establishment of, 5, 25, 45–46, 131
        opposition to, 80–88, 94–96, 102–6, 123–25
        parents, 21
        physical appearance, 75
        as playwright, 154–55
        in prison, 13, 61, 66–68, 115, 121, 133
        on racial pride, 5, 38–42, 53, 126–29, 131, 169
        School of African Philosophy, 16
        trial, 11, 26, 61–65, 125, 132–33, 139
        White America on, 97–101, 137–40
        See also Universal Negro Improvement and Conservation Association and African Communities League (U.N.I.A.)
Garvey, Sarah, 1, 20
"Garvey: a Mass Leader" (Frazier), 118–22
Garvey and Africa (Manoedi), 94–96
"Garveyism and African Nationalism" (Langley), 148–53
"Garveyism in Jamaica" (Lewis), 154–60
General G. W. Goethals (ship), 12
Ghana, 143, 146, 161, 167
Gladstone, Herbert John, 49
Gold Coast, 93
Great African Army, 120
Great Britain, 2–3, 13, 15–16, 55, 69, 87, 92–93, 141–43, 155–57, 159
Great Depression, 69, 157
Guinea-Bissau, 165

Hampden, John, 49
Harding, Clarence, 163–66
Harris, G. E., 137
Harvard Historical Studies, 130
Hawse, Percy, 116
Hodgkin, Thomas, 149, 152
Hood, Solomon Porter, 115
Hughes, Langston, 128
Huss, John, 110

India, 157
International Workers of the World, 142
"Interview with the Reverend Clarence Harding," 163–66
Ireland, 157
Italy, 69, 155
Ivory Coast, 55

Jamaica, 1–3, 14–15, 69, 80–81, 123, 143, 154–60, 167–68

James, C. L. R., 142
Jefferson, Thomas, 59
Jobs for Negroes Campaign, 128
Johnson, Charles S., 128
Johnson, Henry Lincoln, 125
Johnson, Jack, 148
Johnson, James Weldon, 104, 123–25, 153

Kanawha (ship), 7, 10–11, 62, 84
Kenyatta, Jomo, 142, 146
King, Charles Dunbar Burgess, 87, 90, 95, 151
King, Martin Luther, Jr., 168
Kingston Gleaner, 143, 155
Kiwanis clubs, 118, 119
Knight, A., 24
Ku Klux Klan, 57, 59–60, 116–19

Labor unions, 2, 57–59
Labouret, M., 152
Lagos, Nigeria, 150–51
Langley, Jabez Ayodele, 148–53
League of Nations, 14, 155, 157
Lenin, Nikolai, 49
Lewis, Rupert, 154–60
Liberia, 9, 12–13, 55, 74, 76, 87, 90, 92, 95–96, 115, 125, 127, 133–34, 135, 137–38, 151, 163, 169
Liberian Register, 149
Liberian West Africa, 149
Liberty Hall, Harlem, 5, 47, 73, 74
Lincoln, Abraham, 59, 65
Luther, Martin, 110

McCormack, T. A., 24
McGuire, George Alexander, 9, 107–11
McKenzie, Arthur, 24
Madison Square Garden, 8, 25
"Madness of Marcus Garvey, The" (Bagnall), 102–6
Malcolm X, 167
Manoedi, M. Mokete, 94–96
"Marcus Garvey" (Du Bois), 80–88
"Marcus Garvey, Pan-Negroist: the View from Whitehall" (Weisbord), 141–43
Marcus Garvey Memorial Institute, Monrovia, 163, 164
Maugham, R. C. F., 92–93
Minor, Robert, 112–17
Mirabeau, Comte de, 49
Monrovia, Liberia, 9, 163
Morocco, 157
Moton, R. R., 86

Murdock, J. R., 24

Nacion, La, 80
National Association for the Advancement of Colored People, 51, 54, 55, 67, 80, 97, 100, 102, 105, 119, 123–24, 130, 139
National Congress of British West Africa, 143, 150–51
National Urban League, 119
Negro Factories Corporation, 7
Negro Times, 19
Negro World, 5, 7–9, 14, 19, 25, 43, 45–46, 77, 103–6, 120, 121, 127, 131, 132, 134, 142, 148, 149, 151, 152, 155
New Jamaican, 19, 155
"New Nation in Harlem, A" (Tuttle), 73–79
New York Age, 149
New York Times, 133
Nigeria, 89–91, 93, 143, 150–52
Nigeria: Background to Nationalism (Coleman), 143
Nigerian Youth Movement, 143
Nkrumah, Kwame, 143, 145–48, 161, 165
North and East River Steamboat Company, 84
Nyerere, Julius, 165

Opportunity, 128
Organization of African Unity, 165
Ovington, Mary White, 59
Owen, Chandler, 83

Padmore, George, 145, 147
Pan-African Congresses, 119, 131, 134, 144–46
Pan-Africanism, 126, 131, 134, 144–47, 149
See also African redemption, program of
Pan-Africanism or Communism? (Padmore), 145, 146
"Pan-Africanism and 'Pan-Africanism': Some Historical Notes" (Shepperson), 144–47
Panken, Judge, 103
Paul, Saint, 108–9
Peart, A., 24
Peart, Mrs. A., 25
People's Political Party, 15, 156, 158–59
Phillips, Connie, 25
Philosophy and Opinions of Marcus Garvey (ed. Amy Jacques Garvey), 19, 27, 30, 38, 43, 47, 51, 57, 61, 97, 107, 143, 146, 148, 161, 169
Phyllis Wheatley (ship), 11

Pitt, William, 49
Powell, John, 97–101, 116

Quenum, Kojo Tovalou, 151

Race riots, 4, 5
Racial pride, 5, 38–42, 53, 126–29, 131, 169
Randolph, Phillip, 83, 102, 112
Reid, E. E., 24
Reid, J. M., 24
Religion, 9, 107, 121
Rogers, Ben F., 130–34
Rogers, Henry H., 7
Rogers, J. A., 127
Rosenwald, Julius, 59
Ruwa Chiri, Bro., 163–66

Saramacca (ship), 14
Savonarola, Girolamo, 110
Schomburg, Arthur, 127
School of African Philosophy, 16
Sekyi, William Essuman Gwira, 152–53
Senegal, 151
Shadyside (ship), 7, 10, 62, 81, 84
Shepperson, George, 144–47, 149
Sierra Leone, 55, 90, 92–93, 151, 169
Smikle, Thomas, 24
Smith, Alfred E., 14
Socrates, 110
"Some New Light on the Garvey Movement" (Brisbane), 126–29
Spingarn, Joel, 59
Stehazu, James, 149
Suppression of the African Slave Trade, The (Du Bois), 130
Swaziland, King of, 148

Taylor, Marclam, 80
Trinidad, 156
Tropical Africa, 144
Trotsky, Leon, 49
Turner, Henry McNeil, 138
Tuskegee Institute, 3, 20
Tuttle, Worth, 73–79
Twentieth Century Fund, 144

United States Shipping Board, 11, 12
Universal Negro Improvement and Conservation Association and African Communities League (U.N.I.A.)
    aims and objects, 51–56, 76, 81
    branches in West Africa, 150–52
    Communist view on, 112–17
    establishment of, 3, 4, 20, 22–23
    growth of, 5, 25
    in Jamaica, 3, 15, 155, 160
    Liberian colonization project, 9–10, 12–13, 76, 87, 90, 92, 115, 133–34, 135, 138, 151, 163
    in London, 15, 69
    manifesto, 24–25
    modern, 163–64, 167
    1920 convention, 7–9, 25, 30, 73, 81–82, 145
    1921 convention, 47, 73–79
    1922 convention, 11
    1924 convention, 12, 13
    1926 convention, 13
    1929 convention, 14–15, 155
    1934 convention, 15, 155
    Socialist view on, 117
    See also Black Star Line
Up from Slavery (Washington), 3, 22

Villard, Oswald Garrison, 59
Voltaire, 49

"W. E. Burghardt DuBois as a Hater of Dark People" (Garvey), 134
Warnaffe, Ch. du Bus de, 145
Washington, Booker T., 3, 20, 22, 23, 53, 118, 128, 130
Washington, George, 49, 65
Washington Bee, 149
Webber, Francis, 151
Weisbord, Robert G., 141–43
Weller, Royal A., 133
"White America" (Cox), 97, 99
White America Societies, 60
Wiggs, John, 136
"William E. B. DuBois, Marcus Garvey, and Pan-Africa" (Rogers), 130–34
Wilson, H. W., 93, 151
Woodson, Carter G., 127
Wright, C. A., 137

Yarmouth (ship), 6, 10, 25, 61–62, 81, 84, 87, 104–5

Zimbabwe, 165

GREAT LIVES OBSERVED

Gerald Emanuel Stearn, *General Editor*

Other volumes in the series:

THE AMERICAN TORY
edited by Morton and Penn Borden

BISMARCK
edited by Frederic B. M. Hollyday

BLACK RECONSTRUCTIONISTS
edited by Emma Lou Thornbrough

JOHN BROWN
edited by Richard Warch and Jonathan F. Fanton

JOHN C. CALHOUN
edited by Margaret L. Coit

CATHERINE THE GREAT
edited by L. Jay Oliva

CHURCHILL
edited by Martin Gilbert

CROMWELL
edited by Maurice Ashley

DEBS
edited by Ronald Radosh

W. E. B. DU BOIS
edited by William M. Tuttle, Jr.

FREDERICK DOUGLASS
edited by Benjamin Quarles

ELIZABETH I
edited by Joseph M. Levine

HENRY FORD
edited by John B. Rae

FREDERICK THE GREAT
edited by Louis L. Snyder

GARIBALDI
edited by Denis Mack Smith

WILLIAM LLOYD GARRISON
edited by George M. Fredrickson

GOMPERS
edited by Gerald Emanuel Stearn

HAMILTON
edited by Milton Cantor

HITLER
edited by George H. Stein

JEFFERSON
edited by Adrienne Koch

JESUS
edited by Hugh Anderson

LA FOLLETTE
edited by Robert S. Maxwell

LENIN
edited by Saul N. Silverman

LLOYD GEORGE
edited by Martin Gilbert

HUEY LONG
edited by Hugh Davis Graham

MacARTHUR
edited by Lawrence S. Wittner

JOSEPH R. McCARTHY
edited by Allen J. Matusow

MAO
edited by Jerome Ch'en

MARIA THERESA
edited by Karl A. Roider, Jr.

JOHN MARSHALL
edited by Stanley I. Kutler

NAPOLEON
edited by Maurice Hutt

PETER THE GREAT
edited by L. Jay Oliva

ROBESPIERRE
edited by George Rudé

FRANKLIN DELANO ROOSEVELT
edited by Gerald D. Nash

THEODORE ROOSEVELT
edited by Dewey W. Grantham

STALIN
edited by T. H. Rigby

TOUSSAINT L'OUVERTURE
edited by George R. Tyson, Jr.

TROTSKY
edited by Irving H. Smith

NAT TURNER
edited by Eric Foner

**DENMARK VESEY:
THE SLAVE CONSPIRACY OF 1822**
edited by Robert S. Starobin

BOOKER T. WASHINGTON
edited by Emma Lou Thornbrough

GEORGE WASHINGTON
edited by Morton Borden

WILSON
edited by John Braeman